The Secrets of the Eternal Book

THE MEANING OF
the stories of
THE PENTATEUCH

The Secrets of the Eternal Book

THE MEANING OF
the stories of
THE PENTATEUCH

Laitman
Kabbalah
Publishers

by: Semion Vinokur

The Secrets of the Eternal Book: The meaning of the stories of the Pentateuch

Published by Laitman Kabbalah Publishers
www.kabbalah.info   info@kabbalah.info

1057 Steeles Avenue West, Suite 532,
Toronto, ON, M2R 3X1, Canada

2009 85th Street #51, Brooklyn, New York, 11214, USA

Printed in Canada

ISBN: 978-1-897448-84-7
Library of Congress Control Number: 2013936210

Translation: Mark Berelekhis
Proofreading: Mary Miesem
Copy Editor: Claire Gerus
Layout: Baruch Khovov
Cover: Galina Kaplunovich, Inna Smirnova
Executive Editor: Chaim Ratz
Printing and Post Production: Uri Laitman

FIRST EDITION: JANUARY 2014
First printing

CONTENTS

A NECESSARY FOREWORD

Dear reader

If you have ever wondered about the mystery of life, even for a moment contemplated the meaning of existence, or dreamed of finding the "elixir of immortality," hold tight to this book; it is for you.

The Secrets of the Eternal Book reveals how to properly read the Pentateuch, how to break through the outer shells—the mundane actions of this world that the book seems to recount—and discover what really stands behind it all.

Let's start by listing all five books: Genesis, Exodus, Leviticus, Numbers, and Deuteronomy. Those are the translated titles in English, while in the original Hebrew they are *Beresheet* (In the Beginning), *Shemot* (Names), *Vayikra* (And He Called), *Bamidbar* (In the Desert), *Devarim* (Words).

When you pick up the book and start to read, little do you know that its content is encrypted. You read and regard the information as a collection of stories, occasionally stopping to wonder what all the fuss is about. The Pentateuch is the foundation for all of Judaism, Christianity, and Islam, and cited continuously by sages, philosophers, writers, and... politicians. But what is so special about it? Allow me to reassure you that if you aren't satisfied with regarding this book as a historical epic, there is nothing wrong with you. It is a sign that you're searching for the hidden meaning; and if you're really searching, you will invariably find it.

You bombard knowing, authoritative persons with your questions, but they are unable to enlighten you. You read mountains of literature, but cannot seem to find any answers.

You are searching for the code of this book, trying to unearth some secret door through which to sneak in and discover the inner workings of this code. For millennia, scholars have been trying fruitlessly to solve the mystery of this code. Yet, they have been trying to solve it with reason, and this has been their downfall. You cannot crack this code with reason, so don't even bother trying.

To reveal the secrets of the Pentateuch, you need only one "tool"—desire. It is a magical word, and one that we'll be coming back to time and time again.

So where do you begin if you've resolved to delve into the depths of life's foremost question? You open up the book and say to yourself: "This is about me. Everything written here reveals my path into the innermost depths of my soul."

True, the trails have become winding over time. For as long as you can remember, you have only concerned yourself with the outside world: lamenting the chronic lack of money, job dissatisfaction, unrequited love, betrayal, bad food, and the fallibility of public transportation, while rejoicing over purchases of a new house, a new car, new furniture, eating a good meal, watching a good movie... And all things considered, this would be enough for me.

And then something happened... You found yourself increasingly beset with thoughts that all these pleasures were transient and vain. You couldn't resign yourself to the idea that the human being—this phenomenal fusion of intellect and heart—was born into this world only to gratify the body and disappear forever.

All of a sudden, thoughts that life could go on forever began to permeate your mind.

Where have they come from? It sounds too much like science fiction, but... Could it be that your intuition is right? It is. You can, in fact, live forever.

These thoughts come to you from your deepest point. There, hidden deep inside you, is a place where eternity resides. It calls to you endlessly, explaining that all the rest is but empty husks.

You didn't hear its voice until you were ready. It protected you from such profound contemplations, like a child who is given toy cars to play with, until time nurses it to maturity and seats the now grown person behind the wheel of a real car.

The same is true for you. You were a full-grown child. For many years, even millennia, you've "played with toy cars," and then suddenly grew aware of the question inside of you: "Is this really what I'm living for?"

And that was it. The moment you acknowledged this question, you stopped being a child.

And now is when you truly need this book—the veritable roadmap for those who ask themselves the questions about the meaning of life. It's a user's manual to opening the door into the spiritual world that exists within you, a world that is eternal, full of serenity and joy. This world is the source of light in your life.

WHAT IS THE PENTATEUCH?

As we've already mentioned, the first five books of the Bible are called The Torah, in Hebrew (from the word *Horaa*, which means "Instruction," or from the word *Ohr*—"Light"). When it comes to advancing upward along the ray that had been sent down into the darkness of our world, the Light is your manual. Your job is only to "grab it and hold tight." As you set out to follow the instructions in this manual, the spiritual world begins to open up before you, revealing the answers to all your questions. As you cleanse of all things superficial, you begin to clearly see reality gradually changing around you. You realize that all your life you've been asleep, all the while thinking you were awake. You realize that all the things you used to deem valuable are, in fact, immaterial. All that you thought true is actually false, and all the earthly pleasures cannot compare to what awaits you.

If you haven't yet come to this view, just hold on to that one thought: "This book is about me," and you will. Be relentless as you search for it inside yourself, and behind the stories of the forefathers you will reveal the story of your self. Between the lines on the pages of the book you will discover new words, as a special spiritual force begins to reveal itself behind every letter, every symbol and punctuation mark. And you will actually feel the Light gathering and looking for a way to enter into you—not into your physical body, which is worthless, but into your soul, which is eternal.

When the Light enters and begins to cleanse you, all the things that seemed too fantastic and unreal to you before will become clear, evident, and natural.

After one month of reading the book correctly, you will see just how many changes you'll undergo. You will hardly recognize yourself and your inner world. Your world will become whole. You will begin to see and feel that the book is about your soul, which is called Noah when on one level, Abraham on another, Moses on another still, thus proceeding toward Eternity.

And now, if you are ready, we will begin our tale.

A Brief, but Important Preface

More than 5,000 years ago in Mesopotamia, a place that gave rise to many of today's civilizations, there lived a man called Abraham. Nearly all religions and spiritual factions recognize him as their founder and patriarch. They record his name into their holy writings as the first man to reveal the Law behind the world's existence, the first man to attain the Upper Governance.

It is none other than Abraham who is the forefather of the science that transcends nationality, a science that is universal, for it emerged before the world was split into nations and languages. It is a science that has disappeared many a time over the centuries, but always reappeared, ever more wrapped in myths and legends.

This process was deliberate. People were not yet ready to accept it, as it is precisely in our time that this science, known as "Kabbalah," is meant to be revealed. Why is that? It is written about a time when egoism in our world reaches its final phase of development and becomes so powerful that humanity will be unable to control it, needing a remedy to save itself from the ego. It is then that the wisdom of Kabbalah will appear.

The word "Kabbalah" translates as "reception." In other words, it is a science about how to receive correctly, or how to properly utilize one's egoism to receive all the pleasures prepared for humanity.

Kabbalah takes nothing on faith. It invites you to "taste and see that the Creator is good." Dear reader, I call your attention to this once more: "taste and see" does not mean you should agree with something that somebody tells you. You yourself must acquire the sensation of the Creator, and Kabbalah is here to help you do just that.

Therefore, brace yourself, for as you ascend level by level, you will experience all kinds of situations. On every level, you will give the Creator different names, depending on how near or far you are from Him. On one level, you will call him Ruthless; on another, Just; on yet another, Merciful, or Unified, and so forth, and all because you will feel Him as such. Every level brings a new Name for the Creator.

Indeed, the same thing is true for our lives here. For example, when we first meet a person we may call him "reserved." As we get to know him and warm up to him, we may say, "No, it's just that he knows a great deal." Befriend him even more and we deem him wise, then kind, and finally–friendly... even though we began the process with "reserved!" Our assessments change as we reveal his qualities. That person has always been this way; we simply needed to get to know him better. It is very important for our advancement to understand that it wasn't the person who changed, but that we have opened up to him, as if absorbing him within us.

The same is true for the Creator. The better we get to know Him, the more of His qualities we attain, i.e., His names. This happens when we literally live through the contents of the Five Books of Moses, as we let the text flow through us. In this manner we attain the Creator's names as we proceed through the books. With every level—a new name. How long will this process take? Until we discover all the names of the Creator, join Him and attain Him as the absolute Law of Love.

THE LANGUAGE OF THE BRANCHES

Kabbalah has developed its own language. It is called "the language of the branches."

The reason for this is that nothing in our world is accidental. On the contrary, everything was created and is governed with purpose and intention.

The universe, rocks, plants, animals, and humans, all that has happened, is happening, and will happen comes from the Creator, passes through all the spiritual worlds and manifests in our world.

Let us also jump ahead a bit and mention that the Creator has a system of governance over our world. It is called "the world of *Atzilut*," which translates as "At His place." "His" means the Creator's.

The world of *Atzilut* is like a brain, as without its command, nothing ever happens in our world, nothing, not a single thought or action, war or scientific discovery, absolutely nothing... as it is written, "not an insect crawls" or "a blade of grass moves" without His bidding.

Our universe, which can be likened to a giant computer, is governed by the world of *Atzilut*.

That is to say, everything that exists in our world necessarily originates in the Upper World, then descends along the spiritual degrees. There is a rigid connection between the objects in our world and their roots in the Upper World, which may be dubbed their "spiritual doubles." Thus, our world is a consequence of the spiritual world.

Kabbalists feel this very clearly because they exist in both worlds. That is, they see the Upper Object—the root from which everything arises, and its offshoot in our world—the branch.

Because we call the root by the name of its corresponding branch, and not the other way around, the language of Kabbalah is called "the language of the branches," and not "the language of the roots."

With the language of the branches, the Kabbalists have found a way to convey precise information about the spiritual world using the language of our world.

They take the name of an object in our world, say a "tree," and use it to describe its Upper Counterpart, i.e., the force that is now called "tree."

But what if a person doesn't know that the Old Testament was written in this special language? What does he see in it then?

He sees a narrative about our world, about a tree that grows in paradise or a serpent that whispers sweet temptations in Eve's ear.

But this is absolutely incorrect. Such interpretations reduce this book, which is meant to unite our world with the spiritual world, to the level of earthly literature.

(I remember my grandmother sewing cloths with beautiful vivid patterns. Being a child, I would feast my eyes on them and think, "This is how the world is." That was until I happened to look on the back of the embroidery and see a chaotic tangle of threads and knots. At least it appeared chaotic at first glance. Later I understood that that was the root of the beauty. That if you cut even a single knot off the reverse, the entire beautiful pattern would come apart...)

So here we are, wanting to learn to address the root. We see the pattern on the front, comprised of simple, worldly words, but we want to know what is behind them.

As we read the Bible, we will learn to look behind the words and see the forces that are their roots. Moreover, the very intention to read this Book precisely in this manner will already connect us to the Upper World. That is because everything begins with the goal and intention of the reader. From the very first lines, the Bible sets one simple goal: to tell humankind how to become citizens of the spiritual world. It wants to lead us to the Creator, to eternity, to happiness. And whoever reads it must fashion the same intention: "I am doing this in order to reveal the Creator."

And now let us begin our journey toward the secrets of the greatest Book of all nations and generations. Are you ready? Off we go! The first chapter of Genesis is called *Beresheet* in Hebrew, and translates as: "In the Beginning."

CHAPTER 1

IN THE BEGINNING
(GENESIS, *BERESHEET*)

"In the beginning God created the heaven and the earth. And the earth was unformed and void, and darkness was upon the face of the deep; and the spirit of God hovered over the face of the waters."

Interpreting these words literally can spark the mind to imagine what the Creator looks like, how He "moves," "talks," "sees"... There is unlimited room for fantasy: waters, darkness, face of the deep...

But who needs these fantasies? Those who are trapped by the desires of our physical world, who want to learn but not attain, who like to contemplate and argue, especially if there's someone around to listen.

If you are still satisfied with the pleasures of this world, then go ahead and enjoy music, art, and any other delight this world can offer. But if you want to attain the spiritual world, you should be concerned with something altogether different—you need the Creator.

If you need answers to questions that will not leave you alone, if you want to know why you were born, the purpose of this vast universe we live in, it means only one thing: that you will not rest until you get to the bottom of the mystery that is your soul.

And if that's the case, well, that is a completely different story. It means that you have already begun to ascend the spiritual ladder.

Before you awaits the highest rung one can attain. It is *Beresheet*—the opening chapter of the Book of Genesis. The highest state described therein can only be attained at the end of correction.

"In the beginning God created the heaven and the earth." This passage speaks of the creation of the Upper World—a space wherein your soul will exist. Your "I" is not yet awake; you do not yet perceive your own existence. Only the habitat is created—the Supernal Mother in whose womb you will be conceived.

So what is this habitat? I will jump ahead a bit and say this: the words "created" and "in the beginning" allude to the creation of two qualities—egoistic and altruistic—between which your soul will soar.

"...the earth was unformed and void." Here is where the spiritual terms make their first appearance. The word "earth" in Hebrew is *Eretz*, from the word *Ratzon*—desire. Therefore, earth stands for desire. From here on we will only be dealing with desire, because desire determines everything.

"...the earth (desire) was unformed and void." It follows that the desire was not yet formed (unformed and void), meaning we had no desire to reveal the spiritual world.

So what was there? Only a clean sheet of paper ready to record the history of humankind, the history of the one soul. That is what the passages allude to—the very beginning, when the spiritual world was conceived within you. In other words, in this chapter we are beginning to examine the conjunction of forces that arose first. They formed the world within which man (Adam, your spiritual "I") later appears. They created the habitat that man will inhabit. "Man" is the spiritual desire that springs up within.

You may ask: "If these forces are within me, why is it that I cannot sense them?!"

Well, first of all, can you sense how your organs work, such as how your stomach digests food, how your lungs breathe? No, you can't.

These processes fully determine your physical subsistence, yet you do not sense them.

The same principle applies here. Your spiritual life is formed by tumultuous processes that you do not sense until you begin to feel an overwhelming desire to become a participant, or better yet, the protagonist in this wondrous play.

This is how your soul is formed. Working on you now are your Great Grandfathers—the forces of the world of *Atzilut*. Your time has come—the time for you to be born. Sooner or later, when you traverse all the degrees of correction, you will come to meet your "relatives." But in the meantime, you must be patient.

A black, impenetrable screen separates you from everything that transpires on the inside; you cannot see or otherwise sense anything through it. It has been growing thicker over a long time (to use earthly wording), rendering you increasingly egoistic and interested in external, rather than internal matters. More and more, you grew concerned with your body, rather than your soul. Just think back to all the desires that sprang up inside you through your life, and how far from spirituality they were.

The screen grew thicker with layer upon layer, smothering the spiritual desires within you until you found yourself at a dead end. "What surrounds me? Bodies upon bodies. They eat, make money, propagate... What lies ahead of me? Death? But if that's the case, then what is the purpose of my existence?"

These are the questions that prompt one to embark on the path "back to the sources," to *Beresheet*, "the beginning." In reality this path leads to the Light. You ascend toward the forces that govern the world. Every spiritual degree along the path is a mystery: "What other great surprises does the Creator have in store for me?"

This is how we gradually begin to cleanse ourselves of this dark coating called "egoism," for it prevents us from living, breathing, seeing. More and more, we begin to uncover our souls—a complicated mechanism for attaining the spiritual world.

The pleasure we are meant to experience is absolute. It is precisely what the Creator has prepared for us. Herein lies the goal of creation—to fill us, His creations, with the feeling of eternity and perfection. Because the Creator Himself is eternal and perfect, He wants to impart His state to His creations.

Well then, let's not keep Him waiting.

"And God said, 'Let there be light.' And there was light." This is how the spiritual world is created. This is how the forces we spoke of earlier come together and determine the exact residence of the future soul. It will reside in the Light and will be filled by it.

What is the Light? Whatever you do, do not try to envision it. It is a futile undertaking, particularly because our corporeal notions are too narrow to properly define it. We compare the Light to the light of the sun, or a feeling of inner harmony.

The Light is the only thing in existence. It surrounds us—our souls, the whole world, and the entire universe. It is the quality of the Creator, the quality of complete and absolute bestowal. It is the law of Love and Goodness. The Light is all of those things.

And the sooner we realize this, the faster we will surmount all the sufferings of this world, which are given to us for one reason only—to help us realize what we need to "return" to—that same Light of Love.

"And God saw the light, that it was good; and God divided the light from the darkness." If the Light—absolute bestowal, the Creator's great law of altruism—comes into existence, it stands to reason that there must also be someone whom the Creator wants to delight, upon whom He wishes to bestow everything He has.

The role of this "someone" is assumed by Creation.

Creation is us. It is me, the whole world, the world inside of me.

We are the receivers.

And thus, two previously nonexistent states are formed: bestowal—the quality of the Creator (or, the Light), and reception—the quality of Creation.

The passage, "And God divided the light from the darkness," alludes to this process—the forming of two states: the Light and the darkness, the Creator's quality and Creation's quality, bestowal and reception.

This process was included in the very first word of the Book of Genesis—*Beresheet*, which comes from the word *Bar* (Aramaic: outside), meaning Creation's departure from the Creator, its exit from the "bosom" of the Creator.

The word *Beresheet* encompasses the entire path of humankind and the full meaning of the Bible. Included is the understanding that you have exited from the Creator's bosom and must return to Him following a long path of growing egoism that all of humankind must undergo. For that to happen, you must realize that you have truly become distant from the Creator and have immersed yourself in egoism, that you are unwell, and egoism is the cause of your illness.

What is more, the illness of egoism affects the whole world, tearing it into pieces. Only after you've understood this can you embark on the path back to the Creator. As you advance along this path of correcting your egoism, you earn a reward infinitely greater than anything you can imagine— you earn Eternity. You acquire eternal, unbounded bliss. You rejoin with the Creator on a higher level because this unification is *conscious*.

"And God called the light Day, and the darkness He called Night. And there was evening and there was morning, one day." Two states have formed within you: Light—ascent, bestowal, an altruistic quality, and darkness—descent, reception, an egoistic quality. Separating, differentiating between them is your first step toward correction. This state is called "Day One of Creation."

DAY ONE

Every one of us consists of two contrasting qualities: darkness and light, evening and morning. These states represent our spiritual ascents and descents. Ascents and descents have nothing to do with how much money you gained or lost, but with how near or far you are from the Creator, and hence from His quality of bestowal.

Therefore, when the notions of "day-night" and "morning-evening" are mentioned in Genesis, know that they refer to your changing states. The goal in spiritual progress is to find ways to keep the descents short-lived, and swiftly shift to the next phase—one of ascent, of morning.

The secret of good and bad states can be defined by proximity to the Creator: when I am close to His quality of Love, I enjoy a state of ascent, and feel good. The farther I am from this Law, the more I suffer a state of descent, and feel bad. Although I always look to attribute my despair to corporeal factors, like ill health, loss of money, a tiring work day, or a fight with my spouse, these justifications are false. The situation appears that way to me from my uncorrected state, when the root—the force that's really pulling the strings—is concealed from me. Thus, I find myself immersed in my "I," in my egoism, instead of trying with all my might to come out of it.

The truth is that no matter how hard I try, I am powerless to do it. However, this fervent striving is what leads me to the true prayer, found not in the mind but in the heart. This is precisely the prayer the Creator wants from me, one that He answers instantly and without fail.

A "prayer" is a plea, a demand that is born in my heart. It is "inscribed" in it, rather than read in a prayer book. A prayer is my desperate plea for help, for deliverance, an appeal to the Creator, beseeching Him not to abandon me to the bondage of egoism.

When does such a prayer arise? Only when I come to realize that I cannot escape the ego's deadly grip by myself. Only then do I turn to the Creator for help, imploring Him to grant me the necessary strength.

That is precisely the prayer that this Book teaches me. It tells me that all these states are necessary for the development of my soul. There cannot be morning without evening; I cannot feel an ascent if I haven't experienced descent. Hence, together they comprise the whole spiritual desire; together they are "evening and morning," descent and ascent which unite into "one day."

"And there was evening and there was morning, one day." This is the one spiritual vessel, the only one capable of receiving the Light.

So let's recap the "days of Creation" referenced at the very beginning of Genesis. These passages explain precisely what you need to do with your soul on each of the "days." For instance, on the "first day" you need only feel that the Light (quality of bestowal) exists, and that will already trigger the thoughts of what your inner "day and night," "morning and evening" might be. These initial sensations are only beginning to stir within you. An environment is being formed for the soul to reside in, for the human that will arise within you.

DAY TWO

"And God said, 'Let there be a firmament in the midst of the waters, and let it divide the waters from the waters.' And God made the firmament and divided the waters which were under the firmament from the waters which were above the firmament, and it was so. And God called the firmament Heaven. And there was evening and there was morning, a second day."

Don't get caught thinking that everything was filled with water, for the passage speaks of something very different.

The word "water" in Genesis means the Light of Mercy. And the created expanse called "heaven" alludes to the need to separate within me thoughts and desires, so as to see which of them are Light (meaning "heaven"), and which of them are dark. The dark desires are called "earth," but we'll talk more about them later on.

This is the very first commandment you must perform. Only afterwards can the soul be conceived. (Note that here, too, Earth is conceived on the basis of water, that is, on the Creator's quality of mercy.)

"And God said, 'Let the waters under the heaven be gathered together unto one place, and let the dry land appear.' And it was so. And God called the dry land Earth."

This separation of "heaven" and "Earth"— light thoughts from dark thoughts—is called the "recognition of evil." It is a state where you clearly realize that within you lies evil that must be corrected, or you will never reach the spiritual world. And if the desire to obtain the spiritual world lives within your heart, haunting you, you will do whatever it takes to cleanse yourself of this evil. However, your first step is to expose and recognize the evil within.

RECOGNITION OF EVIL

Recognition of evil happens by studying Kabbalah books written by Kabbalists at high spiritual levels. These books contain a special luminescence that you invariably draw by trying to understand the meaning of the texts. Shortly into the study, you begin to feel how opposite you are from this luminescence, which represents selfless love and bestowal. It helps you realize that you are an egoist, always striving to use everyone around for your own benefit.

The luminescence is peace and security, whereas you are consumed with fear and anxiety. The luminescence is eternal, blissful life, whereas you are dragging along in a wretched existence full of suffering, at the end of which comes death.

You want to merge with the Light. You make that your goal, you know that it's possible, but how do you cleanse yourself and become similar to the Light?!

If you continue to apply to yourself all that these books speak of, if you try to realize that they are written for you and about you, it won't be long before you feel the world around you beginning to change. This is the beginning of the process of your purification of evil, your first steps toward the Light.

Yet, this path is fraught with inevitable states of descent. When those moments come, how do you endure and refrain from saying something like, "The goal is impossible; I am too weak and ought to stick to matters of this world; no use dreaming of eternal happiness; I am tired, exhausted."

How do you endure these devastating states? Well, there is a remedy, but for now you must listen to yourself, for your entire spiritual life depends on it. Little by little you will learn to analyze which of your qualities pertains to the spiritual, and which to the animal, which bring you the sensation of life, and which the sensation of death. Your recognition of evil will grow until it becomes absolute. That will be the real breakthrough into the spiritual dimension, a proof that you will be granted a remedy.

BACK TO "THE HEAVEN AND THE EARTH"

Remember the following Kabbalistic concepts, for you will need them from here on: "Heaven" means the quality of bestowal. When acquired, the creature becomes filled with the Light of Mercy—the pleasure of being similar to the Creator.

"Heaven" means the Creator's spark within you, a tiny grain of completely selfless bestowal and love that you discover within. It is precisely this quality of "heaven" that prompts the feeling of unease, compelling you to search insistently for something that doesn't exist in this world.

"Earth" is all of your egoistic desires. This entire world is built on them.

And between these two polar opposites—"the heaven and the earth"—is your soul. Its state is unstable, as though hung on a string.

Subject to these two forces, in times of ascent the soul draws nearer to the heaven, to bestowal, to the Creator, and you feel like you're soaring as joy overcomes you. In times of descent, the soul falls to the ground, to the desires of the body, to egoism, and you are imbued with worldly concerns, calculations, fear for the future, and a total lack of faith.

It is similar to the way we maintain balance as we walk, our legs taking turns: first the right, then the left.

The correction process is the same. You find your "golden mean," that is, you utilize your innate egoistic desire by transforming it into an altruistic one, in order to climb up the spiritual ladder to the Creator, ultimately acquiring His quality of bestowal.

It can further be said that correction constitutes the very understanding that the quality of bestowal exists, that it must be acquired, and that you must work with your egoism—"earth"—to achieve this goal. While previously you didn't have this understanding, now you begin to live and draw closer to Infinity.

Your whole objective is to shorten the period of descent, to not allow it to last for months, weeks, or even hours, but a mere instant.

You must constantly cultivate the "heaven" within yourself. We have plenty of "earth." Being born egoists, our entire lives are filled with "earth." However, we have only a tiny spark of "heaven," and this spark must be kindled.

Think back to your "past" life, where you viewed the surrounding world through the prism of your "healthy" egoism! Back then, any mention of the spiritual world seemed only to distract you from real and worthwhile endeavors.

"I'm working here," you would say, "building a business, making a career, starting a family, and these people are bugging me with their stories of 'heaven'!" That is, in your perception, the spiritual world was barely worth considering.

Today, however, with your vocabulary enriched with new terminology, like "earth," "heaven," "egoism," "bestowal," "life," "death," and "the secret of Creation," the spiritual world has gained significance and become a desired goal. Today, it has truly become a world, and not just a point. You continue to pursue a career, do business, build and maintain your home, but it doesn't detract from your advancement along the spiritual path. You want to live in both worlds, and you understand that this is possible.

Kabbalists differ from other people precisely in their ability to use the altruistic quality of "heaven" to correct the egoistic quality of "earth." In no way do they attempt to suppress or eradicate egoism.

The correction consists of seven states, called "seven days." Naturally, the days in question have nothing to do with our earthly calendar. This correction can occur in a matter of seconds, or stretch over a year, many years, a lifetime, or many lifetimes. It depends only on you.

It is written in Genesis: "And God said, 'Let the waters under the heavens be gathered together unto one place, and let the dry land appear.'"

As soon as your consciousness fills with Light, of thoughts of the Creator and the Upper World, you begin to feel that you are comprised of qualities entirely opposite to the Light. Your qualities are egoistic, i.e., "earthly," hence the phrase, "Let the dry land appear." You begin to think about what can be done to make life appear, for the first sprouts of bestowal to emerge. (This is described in the Book of Genesis as the emergence of living and non-living organisms.) You no longer want to exist as before. You simply cannot allow it. There is a point that has come alive in your heart, a point that is in direct contact with the Creator, and it won't let you rest.

The "heart" symbolizes all the egoistic desires of this world, while the "point in the heart" is the Creator's sprout. It can also be likened to a lifeline that the Creator lowers into our world, so we can grab it and rise to Him.

So how does spiritual life begin on earth? Or, to use the language of Kabbalah, how do I use my egoistic desires (earth) to grow the first sprouts of bestowal within me? How do I break through my egoism and move toward the Creator?

This is done with the help of a special Light that He sends us. Two types of Light emanate from the Creator: "The Light of Life" and "The Light of Mercy." This is precisely how the creature perceives them.

By using the quality of the Light of Mercy, which is called "water," you acquire the ability to bestow. What does this mean in terms of your corporeal life, and how do you achieve it? You must "cleanse" yourself by reading the books composed by those who have already attained the spiritual worlds, writing to us from their heights. In so doing, you draw the emanation of the Upper Light that these books contain.

Herein lies your spiritual work. The very process of reading is already helpful, but if you approach it with the desire to change, to be like the Light, to cleanse yourself of the ego, the Light influences you to a much greater degree. It is precisely this influence of the Light that separates the works of Kabbalists from all the other texts in our world.

That is when "life appears on the earth," meaning you begin to clearly sense the first, tender sprouts of spiritual desires. These desires haven't yet taken a complete hold of you. Rather, your state is like that of a baby who hasn't yet learned to walk, but can already use his feet to kick. Better yet, you are like those first blossoms—unable to move, but which are drawn toward the sun.

When night falls, you wither, for night can be likened to states of descent, which are inevitable and mean only one thing: that you are advancing. (Indeed, obstacles are sent only to those who are advancing. Obstacles are necessary for strengthening one's resolve in order to wage an "inner battle" and come to a genuine prayer: "I know that morning will come, and I ask for the strength to endure, to overcome all the descents. I know that at present I am undergoing a cleansing of my desires, which are resisting, demanding that this process be stopped, appealing to my reason and logic. But I don't want to hear them. Instead, I ask You for the strength to endure...") And then morning invariably comes—a state of ascent, confidence in knowing that you've acted correctly in choosing the spiritual path—and like a flower, you open to the Light.

Let's reiterate. "Earth"—the egoistic quality—is our nature. We already know that "tilling" it must be done carefully. We also know that "water" (Light of Mercy) is our main helper. It corrects the ego, saturates the earth, and facilitates the conditions for new life to be born. "Life" refers to the quality of bestowal; that is, the correct use of egoism—for the benefit of yourself and others.

You may ask, "What is "corrected egoism"? It is a state where you feel bliss from bestowing pleasure upon the people around you, and not from using them for your own pleasure. This bliss can only be felt in such a state, which is characteristic of the spiritual world.

What do you see in our world? Your eyes detect all kinds of objects, plants, and bodies. How do you relate to them? You love them if they bring you pleasant sensations, and you hate them if they don't bring you any pleasure. In other words, your attitude toward them is completely egoistic.

What happens when you correct your egoism, or even when you merely begin the process of its step-by-step correction? You suddenly begin to notice things you hadn't noticed before. Through this imaginary world, you begin to see the real world, one that has always existed around you, a world that is full of Light, Love, and mutual bestowal, the Creator's world, the so-called "world to come."

You have never seen it because you were full of darkness and hatred. It was concealed from you by your own ego.

Your world and "the world to come" have nothing in common whatsoever, as they exist by different laws. Many people carry the false notion that "the world to come" is a place they go to after death.

Not so. "To come" means it is your next state, which you must attain not after death, but in your lifetime, here and now. The moment you put yourself in congruence with "the world to come," you acquire the ability to see it.

It is as if you exit yourself, leave your egoistic body, and open yourself up to a new world, a world with only one law—the Law of Bestowal. And you aspire toward that world because the lives of its inhabitants are founded on mutual love. Thus, instead of perceiving only our world with its bodies and objects, you begin to perceive the force that governs it, to the extent that you grow more similar to this force. By aspiring to bestow, you realize that this force is the absolute good. This force is the Creator.

This is how you come to perceive the pure, genuine Light, just as it stems from the Creator. It is as if you come out to meet the Light before it enters and fills you. This, the Creator's Light, is not yet weakened by your egoistic filters. It is still pure, and you are given the opportunity to feel it. The very fact that you are capable of detecting it is happiness in its own right. This is called, "to hear the Creator's call."

Afterward, when the Light passes through your system of filters, all that remains is a tiny glimmer, so weak that even an uncorrected person can endure it.

It is the same Light that you had felt as your point in the heart. It is what Kabbalists call "a tiny candle."

This Light trickles into our world through the thick wall of egoism that screens it. It enters here with the sole purpose of maintaining life in our world. This Light "hides" within all the objects of our world, dressed in all kinds of garments. All those times you found yourself enjoying good food, new things, fame and money, it was this very Light that drew you toward it! That was the true source of your enjoyment!

You may ask: would anything exist in reality if not for this Light? Our world would not exist. There wouldn't be anyone with the desire to live because there wouldn't be any desires.

However, the very fact that you have a desire (and a great one at that) to attain the depth of what is happening to you speaks of one thing and one thing only (no offense intended): that you are a big egoist, much bigger than everybody else. Whereas others are satisfied with this world, you demand nothing less than the spiritual one! You will not rest until you reveal it, and that is a very good thing because it is precisely what the Creator wants from you.

And this brings us to Day Three—an explanation of your new desires.

DAY THREE

"And God said: 'Let the earth put forth grass, herb yielding seed, and fruit-tree bearing fruit after its kind, wherein is the seed thereof, upon the earth.' And it was so. And the earth brought forth grass, herb yielding seed after its kind, and tree-bearing fruit, wherein is the seed thereof, after its kind; and God saw that it was good. And there was evening and there was morning, a third day."

We already said that after the correction of "water" (Light of Mercy), the "earth" (your desire to receive) becomes fit to bear fruit, as the qualities of water and earth have joined together.

In itself, abundant water is just as destructive for life as is dry earth. Case in point, Noah and the flood.

Man's correction is built precisely on the ideal combination of altruistic and egoistic qualities within his soul, the "heavens" and the "earth," the Creator and the creature.

This correction is called moving along the "middle line." Remember this definition!

Your innate egoistic nature is called "earth," or the left line.

The quality of the Creator, "water," absolute bestowal is the right line.

The middle line is what you must create on your own, by combining the right and the left lines.

That is, you must combine the "water" with the "earth" in a complementary way, which would allow the two qualities to "bear fruit."

You ought to ask for rain and not a storm, since you are not yet capable of bestowing like the Creator. However, you are ready to gradually advance, starting with correcting your smaller egoistic desires, as it is written: "And the earth brought forth grass, herb yielding seed after its kind." Subsequently, rougher desires emerge, as in "and tree bearing fruit, wherein is the seed thereof, after its kind," followed by even rougher desires ... until your eyes fully open to the wonderful world that the Creator has prepared for you.

You ought to "ask for rain" so that these two qualities ("water" and "earth") combine to ultimately grow the "Tree of Life"—a spiritual person who perceives the whole universe, existing eternally and blissfully in all the worlds.

Eternally, because by identifying yourself with an eternal soul instead of a transient body, you begin to equate your being with your soul, relegating the body to its true role—an ephemeral shell that simply accompanies it. This transition to identifying yourself with the soul, rather than the body, is strictly internal, taking place as you gradually acquire the quality of bestowal through working correctly with the Kabbalistic books.

DAY FOUR

"And God said: 'Let there be lights in the firmament of the heaven to divide the day from the night; and let them be for signs, and for seasons, and for days and years; and let them be for lights in the firmament of the heaven to give light upon the earth.' And it was so. And God made the two great lights: the greater light to rule the day, and the lesser light to rule the night; and the stars. And God set them in the firmament of the heaven to give light upon the earth, and to rule over the day and over the night, and to divide the light from the darkness; and God saw that it was good. And there was evening and there was morning, a fourth day."

Reminder: the human being (Adam) inside of you has not yet been born. This excerpt speaks only of creating the environment for his birth and life. What is an "environment"? It is forces—the Creator's forces that will influence the person. They exist only to bring one to the goal of Creation—unification with the Creator and eternal happiness.

So, which forces were revealed on Day Four? "And God said: 'Let there be lights in the firmament of the heaven to divide the day from the night.'"

The lights are to govern "night" and "day"—the states one undergoes on the path to the Creator. I'll bet you've already felt periods of constant ascents and descents—these are the "day and night" in question.

"Day" refers to an ascent, when you are filled with confidence that you are on the right path, flying on the anticipation of the doors into the spiritual world opening up before you any second now. "Night" is a descent, when nothing brings joy and the spiritual world seems nonexistent or made up, and you ask yourself, "Why am I wasting my life on this nonsense?"

These questions are thrown at you by your ego. The ego finds the perfect moment to attack because it knows that if you endure, and break into the spiritual dimension, you will escape its rule. Naturally, the ego doesn't want this, so these common questions abound, "Whom do you work for?" "Can you even see Him?" "Where is your reason?" "Look around, people are leading peaceful and pleasant lives, while you're struggling toward an unrealizable goal!"

Need I go on?

There is only one thing to suggest: when "night" falls, make sure you are surrounded by people like you, who are seeking the path into the spiritual world. Friends who have the same goal as you will bear the brunt of the ego's blow, and you will realize that alone, you are helpless, but together, you will endure.

Another useful advice is to go to sleep. What does it mean to "go to sleep?" It means to disconnect from all the pestering questions, block them out, and not look back. You "sleep" through this period. Hey, it's dark out, anyway. Lie down and sleep so that your head (thoughts, calculations) and body (desires) are on the same level, like an animal. In essence, you don't let anything in.

It's as if you cancel, nullify yourself, waiting it out as you gather your strength. You think no thoughts, make no actions or movements, and rightfully so. You know that morning is right around the corner.

"Morning" signifies a new ascent, a way out of the state of descent.

You may ask, "Why does the Creator send us these ascents and descents? Couldn't He have gifted us with all the goodness, as He plans on doing ultimately anyway, foregoing all the suffering and doubts?" Well, He sends us these states because without them there would be no advancement, as progress is possible only via a continual change of states.

Only by overcoming is a true person born, a real "man." I repeat, we're always talking about what happens within, and there we have "man" and "woman," as well. This notion refers to the "inner man" (Heb. *Gever*, from the word *Hitgabrut*—to overcome).

What would happen if you gave your child everything it wanted? It would not develop, but would grow up spoiled, capricious, selfish, and lacking empathy. Would you be happy with such a child? This is why one must go through all that is destined for one. Every soul has a unique path to the Goal.

Also, if the Creator had placed you in a good state right away, He would crush you with His Light. You'd be deprived of any free choice, having become a slave to that state. Who could refuse absolute happiness?! But the Creator doesn't want a slave of the Light. He wants a friend, an equal, which you can become only if you go through all the states and choose the Creator of your own volition.

Your task is to feel the immortal soul behind the mortal bodies, whereupon all your questions will fade away instantly; then, you will see the goodness emanating from the Creator and His individual attitude toward every soul. He is with us always; we need only trust His guidance, like a child heeding the advice of a loving father. The child knows that it can rely on the father in every way, and trusts itself to his care.

There is a reason why the lights that separate the day from the night, i.e., my states, are in the heavens. "...and let them be for lights in the firmament of the heaven to give light upon the earth."

Heaven refers to your quality of bestowal, the Creator's quality. Because the lights in the firmament of heaven "give light upon the earth" (egoistic desires), egoistic desires are subject to the "heaven," the altruistic quality in us.

"And God set them in the firmament of the heaven to give light upon the earth, and to rule over the day and over the night, and to divide the light from the darkness; and God saw that it was good."

It follows that only the "lights in the firmament of heavens" affect the change of our states, separating them: "...and to rule over the day and over the night, and to divide the light from the darkness."

Let us repeat once more: this Biblical text describes the structure of the universe in which Adam will reside. Adam is the human in you. The firmament, earth, and lights all refer to the altruistic and egoistic qualities within which he will exist.

The Creator will push the human toward attainment of the spiritual world. To this end you need to identify yourself with your inner qualities, with the "human" in you. If you succeed you will pass through all the states that lie ahead together with Him. The "nights" and the "days," the "mornings" and the "evenings" are spiritual states designed to bring you to Infinity, to life in the Upper World.

"...and let them be for signs, and for seasons, and for days and years." Whenever speaking about time, we must refrain from imagining corporeal days, months and years, for there is no time in the spiritual world. How could time possibly exist in infinity?! You are already connected to an eternal, immortal soul, so what room is there for the notion of time?! Indeed, there is no time, but only changing states on the ever upward path along the spiritual ladder.

"Day" embodies a changing state—ascent and descent in the span of one degree ("morning," "day," and "evening" are all "one day") before crossing over to the next degree.

Hodesh (month) derives from the word *Hidush* (renewal)—a return to a former state on a higher level, renewed and more advanced, having already gone through thirty ascents and descents. Each time you are given additional work with your egoism, causing you to fall, overcome, and continue the ascent along the spiritual ladder.

Shanah (year) derives from the word *Lishot* (to repeat), which is like moving along a spiral that returns to the same state on a higher level. Either way, the ascent is constant.

"Days," "months," and "years" are all in you. You "live through" them by correcting newer and increasingly difficult egoistic desires.

Some require a "day" to be corrected, others a "month" or a "year." Nonetheless, the direction remains invariably up.

DAY FIVE

"And God said: 'Let the waters swarm with swarms of living creatures, and let fowl fly above the earth in the open firmament of heaven.' And God created the great sea-monsters, and every living creature that creeps, wherewith the waters swarmed, after its kind, and every winged fowl after its kind; and God saw that it was good. And God blessed them, saying: 'Be fruitful, and multiply, and fill the waters in the seas, and let fowl multiply in the earth.' And there was evening and there was morning, a fifth day."

The Book of Zohar depicts each day of Creation as "erection of halls" within man, the so-called "celestial chambers" (Heb. *Heichalot*—hollow spaces of desires). As the soul's egoistic qualities become corrected, these hollow spaces gradually fill up with the Upper Light. This is what every person subconsciously aspires to. A gradual filling of the hollow spaces brings all souls to a state of complete correction and perfection.

In the chapter, "The Language of the Branches," we spoke about the fact that the Creator's forces are described with words from our language. In the book, *Genesis*, for instance, they are called fish, fowl and so on: "...and let them have dominion over the fish of the sea, and over the fowl of the air." As you read these lines, you should clearly visualize all the actions that you must carry out for your own correction.

Let's look at the word "fish" (*Dag*), which stems from the word *Daaga* (concern). If you see this word in the text, know that it doesn't allude to fish swimming in water (remember, also, that water denotes the Light of mercy), but to concern. What should you be concerned with? Only with growing closer to the Creator. There should be no other concern for you. These desires to enter the spiritual world are precisely what *Genesis* speaks of.

However, for the moment, we must keep in mind that all desires are within us. In their uncorrected form, they appear as objects in our world, but in their corrected form they are the Creator's forces, governed by His Light.

So then, the Fifth Day alludes to the desires to be corrected first and foremost. This is because they are "easier," that is, easier to correct: "...and let fowl fly above the earth in the open firmament of heaven." The "fowl" touches the "ground" (your egoistic nature), rather than "grow" from it, but it is also subject to correction, resting on its egoistic nature: "...and let fowl multiply in the earth."

Such is your path as well, dear reader—to separate within you egoistic desires, to which you can attach an altruistic intention, and thus try to correct them. To do that, first try to simply think about it. Think and read Kabbalistic books, primarily the books of Baal HaSulam, who took all the ancient Kabbalistic sources from the times of Abraham, Moses, and the ARI, and adapted them to our generation.

But let us return to the book, *Genesis*. Here we see that the time has come to correct the more "difficult" desires, which pertain to the "earth." They are as though begotten by it, brought forth from the earth.

New expanses are formed (*Heichalot*—chambers). And as these more difficult egoistic desires are corrected, these hollow spaces fill up with Light.

Then, the Sixth Day arrives.

DAY SIX

"And God said: 'Let the earth bring forth the living creature after its kind, cattle, and creeping thing, and beast of the earth after its kind.' And it was so. And God made the beast of the earth after its kind, and the cattle after their kind, and every thing that creeps upon the ground after its kind; and God saw that it was good."

The Creator created only one desire—to enjoy. However, this desire is so all-encompassing that bringing us all to the end goal right away is impossible. After all, we're talking about infinite bliss, which is precisely the goal of man's creation. So instead, it is done in phases because the desire to enjoy within us divides into myriad smaller desires. By correcting them one at a time, progressing from "easy" to "difficult," we will achieve infinite bliss, the absolute and everlasting fulfillment prepared for us by the Creator.

For those in whom the point in the heart (the striving for spiritual pleasure) has awakened, working with one's desires becomes a fascinating journey into the Upper World.

Genesis proceeds to describe how we overcome the correction phase of "easy" desires, whereupon we must correct the "difficult" ones, which were "brought forth from the earth."

"Let the earth bring forth living creatures after their kind." As you already know, the "human being" within you is being vigorously prepared for birth. In this process, ever newer desires constantly emerge, but for now they aren't used for your personal enjoyment.

"...and God saw that it was good." The word "good" means that the desires are truly pure.

But who can make use of these desires? Only man. So comes his turn, whereby a "human" is born within you.

"And God said: 'Let us make man in our image, after our likeness; and let them have dominion over the fish of the sea, and over the fowl of the air, and over the cattle, and over all the earth, and over every creeping thing that creeps upon the earth.' And God created man in His own image, in the image of God created He him; male and female created He them."

In other words, inside of you, a "human" is born to rule over all other desires: "And let them rule over the fish of the sea and over the birds of the sky and over the cattle and over all the earth, and over every creeping thing that creeps on the earth." All these desires were created exclusively for man.

The "human" inside you is destined to walk a difficult path before he realizes that ruling over them doesn't mean using them for his benefit, for it only harms him and the world. Quite the contrary, these desires must be used exclusively to others' delight, because with respect to the desires of others, all of us are always free, able to clearly separate ourselves from each other.

We will talk more about this later. But for now it is essential to understand that when you begin to feel other souls around you, you begin to feel like the Creator toward them. Herein lies your opportunity to be free, that is, to be like the Creator. Together we will certainly come to this, and will understand what to do so as to delight the Giver.

Let us return to the situation depicted in *Genesis*. Before "the birth of a human within you," you were filled only with the inanimate, vegetative, and animate desires. What does this mean? An inanimate desire is when you want only one thing—to be still and not think of anything, like a rock by the wayside, totally passive, with only a single thought: "Leave me alone." Think back to all the times you were in such a state!

A vegetative desire is when you react to external stimuli, but are not yet able to move from your place, as if tied to the ground (by egoism). You reach for the sun like a flower, that is, you now have an impulse to move, ascend, and descend, like a flower that opens during the day and wilts at night. You begin to ask yourself questions like, "Why do I suffer?" You aspire for the Light, wishing to be "watered." You are concerned only with your own growth, you consume, you are no longer a rock—and that is progress.

An animate desire implies movement and searching for subsistence. At this stage you may connect with others like you, and band into a pack because together it will be easier to acquire food. You are concerned with breeding and raising your progeny.

And then, suddenly, inside of you emerges the most complex and exalted desire that comprises all the others, called the "Man within us."

The word "man" in Hebrew is "Adam."

"Adam" derives from the word *Domeh*—similar, alike.

Similar to whom?

To the Creator.

Similar in what way?

Similar to His qualities.

The Creator's qualities are pure bestowal, absolute and unconditional love. That is precisely what Adam, who perceives the Creator, aspires to and must ultimately become. (We will continue repeating this until these qualities become familiar to us, then understandable, and finally, felt through and through.)

This is what you must become. Only then will you find yourself in Paradise, meaning you'll resemble Paradise and its Master. Further on we will delve deeper into this captivating topic, exploring where Paradise exists within you, and where Adam exists within this Paradise.

It follows that only one who aspires to be like the Creator, and to be born spiritually, can be called Adam ("man," similar to the Creator). This is the person referenced throughout the book. Only those who aspire to this state will learn to read it correctly. The others will look at the narrative and see all kinds of morals and tips for making life comfortable and successful.

Adam is the desire that has emerged within you, the reason why you're continuing to read this text. All the preceding desires no longer satisfy you. Your couch potato days are over; you are no longer drawn to wealth, and you are no longer willing to work tirelessly to acquire veneration or fame.

What does it all mean? A certain point named "Adam" or "the point in the heart" has awakened within you. This point is one with the Creator and wants to be like Him because He is its root.

This is the meaning of the phrase, "Let us make man in our image, according to our likeness" (Genesis 1:26). In the original Hebrew, it is written *Be Tzelem. Tzelem* (image of the Upper One) is the part of the Creator (the Upper Degree), which descends into man's soul and imports into it the Creator's qualities.

In other words, it is the apparatus of the Upper Governance, in charge of all the souls, their paths and order of correction. This managing apparatus is directly connected to man's point in the heart, the Adam in you.

As was already mentioned, the heart represents all of our earthly egoistic desires, while the point in the heart represents the desires aimed at attaining the spiritual world. This point has nothing to do with the heart. It is given to us by the Creator and is present in all of us, only it takes time to awaken.

Why is it only a point? Because the spiritual desires are not yet developed in you. They are like a baby taking its first steps. This is why they are considered a "point."

The "Adam" in you takes his first steps. He is directly connected to the "parents" (the Creator), and cannot survive without this connection. He wants to grow up to be just like his parents.

Through this point, the Creator connects to us and begins to build His image in us, connecting us to His managing apparatus.

What is the purpose of this apparatus? It will provide you with the information about the program of Creation, the path you must traverse. Without perceiving the spiritual worlds, you cannot know what to do, what your next step should be, or what is required of you. This is why you keep making mistakes and suffer for it.

You are like a blind kitten in a vast world. In order for you to acquire the qualities necessary to advance, the Upper Degree must teach you exactly what you need to do and how to do it. For this reason it issues this auxiliary device called *Tzelem*.

This device is implanted in the soul, where it activates all the necessary corrections. This is why it is written that man (Adam) is made in the Creator's image. Man becomes the predominant creature, the crown jewel of Creation.

RESPONSIBILITY FOR THE WORLD

"...and have dominion over the fish of the sea, and over the fowl of the air, and over every living thing that creeps upon the earth."

By correcting your egoistic desires (the still, vegetative and animate), you also correct the entire universe. Remember this statement for now. Soon we will clarify it, and you will see that your work determines everything that happens around you.

Man bears tremendous responsibility over what happens in the world. Because he doesn't yet understand it—living a life driven by beastly desires—he is hardly to blame. When this realization comes, however, the real work for which he was created will begin.

"So what's the deal?" you may ask, "If I start on the path of correction (first of all, there are no ifs—everyone will have to start on this path sooner or later), I will automatically correct everything in my environment." This is true. All the problems we see in Nature simply mirror what's happening within us. The impending ecological catastrophe, contamination of rivers and seas, extinction of species, and extreme weather events are all reflections of us, the egoistic essence that has enslaved us. The whole world is within us, waiting for us to realize that we are responsible for everything that happens in it, and complete our correction.

For instance, let's assume there is a rock, and let's call it "the Creator." This rock comprises a certain percentage of slate, a certain percentage of lime, a certain percentage of gold, and some other minerals. If the rock were shattered, what would be the percentage of the composing elements in each piece? It would be the exact same percentage as in the complete rock. Because each piece is part of the whole, its composition is identical to the entire piece. This is why geologists need only break off a piece of a rock to learn its contents.

Every one of us is a shard from this "rock," the Creator. We are all comprised of the same qualities of love and bestowal that exist in Him, except we have broken off from Him. What was the cause of this rupture? Egoism—a quality that's completely opposite to the Creator.

How do we return to Him? The moment we understand that we are opposite from Him, and wish to return to the Creator, we will immediately embark on the path back to Him. The main objective on the spiritual path is to build the desire for it. However, we must experience this desire thoroughly, to the very end, until it hurts, until we scream with pain!

Desire is the basis for all things in the world, and determines absolutely everything. Your objective is to adhere to the Creator. If you have the desire to do so, you'll begin to escape the slavery of self-love and you'll immediately feel changes in your environment. There will no longer be a need to hold conferences on ecology, or "Green Peace" rallies, worry about endangered species, and so on. Humankind will understand that the buck stops with us. We must rise above the ego and begin the journey to the Creator.

This is the message of all the books written by Kabbalists. And the moment we rise above our egos, everything will change. We will finally understand another universal truth: The Creator created us in His image and likeness, and we have never left this state.

What does "in His image and likeness" mean? It means that the Creator (the quality of bestowal) created the world, which operates under the law of bestowal. Having been made in the Creator's image and likeness, we live in this world and the world exists in us. But it only exists in us to the extent that we observe the law of that world, the law of bestowal.

We existed and continue to exist in the "Garden of Eden." We didn't see or feel any of this because our egos were getting in the way, cutting us off from the true picture while painting a false, egoistic one.

Man sees the world through his inner qualities. If we are corrupt, the world appears to us as such. If we are pure, so the world appears to us.

We've been living a lie, but now we wish to grasp the Truth. If this thought is alive and kicking within us, then off we go to escape the prison of our egos!

DAY SEVEN

"And the heaven and the earth were finished, and all the host of them. And on the seventh day God finished His work which He had made; and He rested on the seventh day from all His work which He had made. And God blessed the seventh day, and hallowed it; because in it He rested from all His work which God has created to do."

All of man's work, the reason for his existence, amounts to acquiring the qualities of the Creator, which are the qualities of bestowal. Man corrects himself through these qualities, and in the process of the correction he ascends along the spiritual ladder toward infinity and perfection, growing closer and closer to the Creator.

What were we doing over the course of the previous six days, the six degrees of correction? We were looking at our egoistic desires through the prism of the quality of bestowal. At every degree we compared ourselves to the Creator and saw that we still had a lot of work to do. In so doing, we seemingly delved into our "I." During the six "days" we progressed from the "easy" desires (from the standpoint of correction) to the more "difficult" ones.

In the language of Kabbalah, these six degrees of advancement are called *Sephirot*, from the word *Sappir* (sapphire), which means "illumination." The names of the *Sephirot* are as follows: *Hesed, Gevura, Tifferet, Netzah, Hod, Yesod.*

Every degree has its own illumination.

A Kabbalist is someone who is connected to the spiritual world, who feels this connection very clearly.

By working with the "easier" egoistic desires, he places himself on the degree of *Hesed*. His objective is to build himself similar to the Creator. He thinks of only one thing: "What can I do to make our communication pleasurable for Him, how do I change my egoistic desire into a desire to bestow? On this degree He is so pure and bestowing. I want to be like Him, and I know that He wants this, too. I cannot achieve this directly because in His Light I am exposed as a true egoist. I understand that this is my nature, so can I circumvent it?"

Following these thoughts, a person seemingly tells the Creator: "You were the One who created me this way, to receive pleasure, so what can I do to receive yet bestow at the same time? For in this lies the true, eternal pleasure for which You have created me, and not for the fleeting egoistic one. What can I do to delight You, like a son who wishes his father to be happy?"

The answer lies in the question itself: To receive so as to give joy. How? By changing the intention. Instead of the typical self-serving intention, I need to form an intention whereby my actions delight the Creator. This is possible only if, at a particular degree (*Hesed*, for instance), you "see" Him. That is, you clearly feel the magnificence of the quality of bestowal, and the utter baseness and barrenness of the ego. If the Creator heeds your pleas and grants you this revelation, you will be able to change your intention. You will desire to be in bestowal, realizing that there is no greater joy for the Creator than this. If that happens, it means that you have built a "screen."

THE SCREEN

The Screen is the force of resistance against egoistic desires. If you acquire this force, you are in perfect shape, headed straight for the Creator. Here I must add that you cannot build the screen by yourself. Rather, it must be obtained by persistently demanding it of the Creator, which is the Upper Degree. The Upper Degree in the spiritual world is the degree directly above your current degree. This degree is the Creator for you. This is how you attain one of the Creator's names (which we talked about earlier).

At each subsequent degree, you will know the Creator better, meaning you will be revealing more and more of His names until you reach the complete revelation of the Maker.

So, when do you acquire a screen? When the Upper Degree feels that you're prepared to do anything to get it. The plea must come from the bottom of the heart: "Give me strength to bestow like You... Help me correct myself, I beg You." If your plea is sincere, you will receive the screen.

That is, you must "correct" the egoistic desire with the intention to bestow. Every day, it is as if you place your "I" in the Creator's "clinic" and ask for the cure—the screen that will enable you to open your eyes and see the true picture of reality. In this clinic, you are given additional egoistic desires with which you must begin to work and feel, to check your attitude toward them, realize how powerful they are, and only then to ask for the screen—the force that can protect you from falling from this degree.

The goal is clear—to correct your ego, which is supplied to you in portions as you ascend upward and mature. Thus, you gradually move from degree to degree. Once you've dealt with one portion of egoism, you are given an opportunity to ascend, to draw closer to the next batch of egoistic desires. And then you begin to work with them, correcting your intention from egoistic to altruistic, so you can say, "I receive and in so doing I am giving You delight." Every degree contains its own work, its own screen, a new name of the Creator.

The Six Days of Creation correspond to the *Sephirot* in the following manner: *Hesed* is the first day, *Gevura* is the second, *Tifferet* is the third, *Netzah* is the fourth, *Hod* is the fifth, and *Yesod* is the sixth.

These six successive corrections, called "the six days of creation," are also the six millennia of Creation, or the six degrees of delving into oneself. Throughout this period, humankind labors arduously to correct its egoism. Incidentally, we're living in the 5770s, the tail end of the sixth millennium.

Now you might ask, "What about the final, Seventh Degree?"

SABBATH, THE SEVENTH DEGREE

The seventh and final degree is called "the complete, independent creature," which wants to receive and perceives itself as a receiver. It is the final phase of every degree. It is also our root.

This degree cannot correct itself, for it is a concentration of egoism, its foundation. Only after it experiences the preceding six corrections (days of creation) does it acquire the ability to "absorb" them within and adopt their qualities.

Therefore, the objective of the "Seventh Day" is to take all that was created and accumulated during the preceding six days and produce a finished, independent creature.

This seventh degree is called "the Sabbath." It is a special day because in this state, the souls are filled with the Upper Light. The only condition is to not interfere with this process, symbolically represented by the laws of the Sabbath. You put down the oars and go with the flow toward the Light. You submit to these laws and thereby keep your ego in the "off" position. It is also written, "He who works for six days will have food on the seventh." This means that if you've worked on your desires through the six degrees, six millennia, you will receive all that's been prepared for you by the Creator. This is the Upper, Divine Light of abundance and delight.

THE SEVEN DAYS OF CREATION

Now let us sum up the seven days of Creation. What should be the result of the correct inner work? The soul will ascend from the egoistic level to one of bestowal. This is achieved by seven consecutive corrections, called the "seven days of the week."

Seven is the Creator's number. The system that governs our world comprises seven parts. For this reason, our world is divided by seven and seventy: seventy nations of the world, seven days a week, seven colors of the spectrum, seven notes of the musical scale, man's soul divides into seventy parts, man's life is calculated by cycles of seventy years, and in the seventh millennium, man receives the reward he has merited.

Again, we are living in the 5770s. What is in store for us during the remaining 220 plus years before the seventh millennium sets in? Are we to just sit there and let them pass? No. We can intervene in this process, which was set off from above to last 6,000 years, and rush it. This intervention has already begun. All the sages specified the same year, 1995, as the year when the process of the world's conscious correction would begin. It is referenced in many texts penned by the great Kabbalists of the past, including *The Book of Zohar*.

Indeed, since 1995 more and more people the world over are embarking on the path of correction.

However, select individuals can undergo this process separately, attaining the Upper World and coming to sense the Upper, perfect reality before others. Moreover, the very path of correction, when navigated consciously and willingly, feels like an extraordinary adventure.

This is our objective in studying the structure and functionality of this system of the universe—to know precisely where and how we can intervene in the process, change something, and achieve immediate correction.

In fact, one cannot directly influence his root, the source from which he stems, because he exists at a lower degree and derives from it.

However, by correcting himself and equalizing his qualities to his root, a person changes the way he perceives what comes from above: instead of never-ending blows, problems, and everyday hardships, he begins to experience bliss, respite, perfection, undivided attainment.

We were made by the Creator with the sole purpose of mastering the Upper World and assuming control over our destiny.

THE UPPER DESIRE

We have reached the moment of birth of "the human within." A new "human" desire has been born within us. Let us take our time and carefully examine this desire and all that it entails.

To this end, we will turn to the ancient oral source that complements the Pentateuch. It is called the Midrash (the Oral Torah). It has been passed down orally from teacher to student for thousands of years. It has reached our time alongside the Old Testament, and is no less revered than its written counterpart.

The following text is taken from the Midrash on the creation of man: "When the Holy One, blessed be He, came to create Adam, the ministering angels formed themselves into groups and parties, some of them saying, 'Let him be created,' whilst others urged, 'Let him not be created.'

"Love said, 'Let him be created, because he will dispense acts of love.' Truth said, 'Let him not be created, because he is compounded of falsehood.' Righteousness said, 'Let him be created, because he will perform righteous deeds.' Peace said, 'Let him not be created, because he is full of strife'...

"The ministering angels said to the Lord: 'Sovereign of the Universe! What is man, that You are mindful of him, and the son of man, that You think of him? This trouble, for what has it been created?'

"'If so,' He said to them, 'Sheep and oxen, all of them, why; why were the fowl of the air and the fish of the sea created? A tower full of good things and no guests—what pleasure has its owner in having filled it?'"

What is the meaning of this passage, which details the Creator's "conversation" with the "angels"? First and foremost, who is the Creator? The Creator is the unified Law of Nature, the Law of Love and bestowal, present within us and all around us. He is immutable and eternal. We don't perceive Him because we live by completely different laws, but the whole purpose of our lives is to reveal Him.

The "angels" are nature's (the Creator's) forces, which obey the Law and are unable to act or think independently. You could say that the angels simply personify the forces that serve the Law of Love and bestowal.

Keep in mind that the Midrash speaks of what has been revealed by the Kabbalists—those who have commenced the correction and discovered the force of bestowal, the Creator.

Naturally, the opposing forces begin to manifest, personifying human nature, which is wholly egoistic and evil.

Imagine flicking on a flashlight in total darkness. As it illuminates your surroundings, you discover that you've been sitting in a cesspool all this time. At first, it may seem as if you would have been better to remain in the dark, but that is not the case. At least now you know the source of the stench, and why you've been so miserable. Our task is to clean up the cesspool, to rein in our egoism. How? That is precisely what the Midrash explains.

It tells us that man is seemingly "suspended" between two opposite forces, existing at a point halfway between good and evil. He balances between them, and these forces act within him. As we often say, "I am between heaven and earth."

So then, within us are forces ("angels") in balance with Nature that speak out "for man's creation" (within us). Then there are "angels" not in balance with Nature that are against man's creation. They "know in advance" that man will use them for evil, harming himself and the whole world. That said, keep in mind that all these forces—the angels who speak for and against—are the Creator's forces. All this hullabaloo was conceived by the Creator for a single purpose: so we would independently choose the side we're on.

Man is born an egoist. From the very beginning, he is mired in imbalance and prefers falsehood to truth. This is why the quality of truth, called "the Creator's seal," objects to man's creation. This is for his own good—to prevent him from suffering, since he is not balanced with the general law.

"Truth said, 'Let him not be created, because he is compounded of falsehood.' Righteousness said, 'Let him be created, because he will perform righteous deeds.'"

Precisely because man is an egoist, he will have the opportunity to realize this, and then to show mercy. Thanks to his good deeds he'll be able to realize what is good, so that afterward he can acquire the quality of bestowal and correct himself. It is as if this "angel" says, "All of man's qualities will be corrected because I exist within him, so don't worry."

But there is also the "angel of peace."

"Peace said, 'Let him not be created, because he is full of strife.'" He protests because man is opposite to peace. He lives for himself and his only thought is to possess everything. And if everybody only wants to receive for themselves, shamelessly taking advantage of others, what kind of peace could there be?

Man is aggressive, delights in the misery of others, strives to harm others, and longs to hoard more than necessary for his existence. The evil qualities in him elevate him above the animate degree, but while the animate degree is in harmony with Nature, man is not!

The lion and the cow take from their environment only what they need for their sustenance, but man does not. Nature dictates this behavior in animals, but not in man. There is not a single quality in man that he uses to achieve peace. The notion of peace means the following: *I take only what I need to survive; the rest does not belong to me.*

He is born with a grotesque desire to rule and dominate the whole world to suit his needs, which is contrary to Nature's quality of bestowal. This is why the angel of peace speaks so vehemently against man's creation, for he brings only discord and war to the world.

And, indeed, we see that the history of humankind is a procession of wars. If man were to grow cognizant of his essence, he would realize that all he thinks of is how to use others for his own benefit. This is what we mean by "war": perpetual takeover of another's territory, i.e., the enslavement of another's "I" by my own.

The whole progress of humankind throughout millennia amounts to the development of weapons of mass destruction. Man sought ways to rule, profit, and use his strengths by elevating himself over others. This is why the angel of peace is right in saying that man is all discord. Not one of his inclinations is directed toward achieving balance with his environment, which would allow him to give others their due. Instead, man strives to acquire and control everything that belongs to others.

The Midrash states that in this form, man shouldn't even come into the world. The reason is clear: the Midrash is an instruction that "lives" within man, but he resists it and doesn't want to live according to its instruction. Therefore, the angels that oppose man's creation are initially correct. Given the circumstances, man should not be created, for he is opposite to all of Nature.

However, when man uses his powers correctly and achieves correction, he becomes king over Nature and the world, the whole process becomes purposeful, and man becomes equal to the Creator.

It was already mentioned that the Creator is the all-encompassing law of Nature, which includes all the "angels," namely forces and particular laws. The Creator says to them, "Nevertheless, I am for creating man, despite his flaws, because I see that through this process he will obtain a spiritual degree. That is what I need from him. He will correct himself. He will rid himself of his ego and come to Me. And when he does, it will be of his own accord, not as a slave to My Light. This is very important."

Thus, the Creator doesn't mind the initial state of Creation and all the states we go through. He already sees us in the final state, which is the reason for our existence.

The struggle described in the Midrash is ever-present within man. With every step, at every moment in life, man works to establish this balance, and thereby brings balance to the whole world. He cannot stand still, for every state compels him to act, and he chooses his path with each step. Every second, man must connect to the goal of Creation, scrutinizing why the Creator had chosen to make him, despite all the forces and qualities that opposed his creation. Indeed, the goal of man's work lies in justifying his own creation.

This is what happens in every one of us; we only need to be sensitive to it.

WHAT MAN WAS MADE OF

The Creator wished to make the body of Adam. This is how He worked: To fashion the hands and legs of Adam, the Creator gathered earth from all the corners of the world. For his torso, He took the earth of Babylon. To fashion Adam's head, the most important part of the human body, He took the earth of *Eretz Ysrael* (The Land of Israel). The Creator put all the gathered earth atop Mount Moriah, where the sacrificial altar shall be in the Temple. He mixed it with water taken from all the oceans of the world, and from the resulting clay He fashioned the body of man.

Clearly, the Midrash isn't speaking of how the biological human body was made, or about mixing clay and earth with water, like children playing with a bucket and spade, or potters shaping clay into pottery. Rather, the Midrash describes how man includes within him all of the world's forces. Here is what is written, "To fashion the hands and legs of Adam, the Creator gathered earth from all the corners of the world." This means that man contains the desires of the whole world ("earth from all the corners of the world"). If he corrects them, he will thus correct the whole world.

"He mixed it with water taken from all the oceans of the world, and from the resulting clay he fashioned the body of man." The "water" in man represents the force of bestowal, the quality of altruism, which animates everything, which is also collected from the whole world.

Thus, both the desire to enjoy (earth) and the desire to bestow (water) exist in abundance in man. They are mixed and connected together in man's every desire. We need only identify the force of bestowal and use it to correct the force of reception, so that bestowal will dominate reception. Then all our desires to enjoy, gathered within us from all the "nations" of the world, will be activated only by the quality of bestowal.

"To fashion the head of Adam, the most important part of the human body, He took the earth of *Eretz Ysrael* (The Land of Israel)."

The Creator made man's "head" out of the "earth" of Israel, out of desires aimed at the Creator. Thus, all of man's aspirations must be aimed at acquiring the Creator's qualities. Israel comes from the words *Yashar El*, which translates as "straight" (*Yashar*) and *El* (to the Creator).

The Creator took the "earth" for man's "torso" from Babylon, the degree that pertains to the quality of bestowal. It is no accident that Babylon was the setting for a great crisis known as "the Tower of Babel." The Babylonians wanted to attain Godliness with the help of the forces of reception, and this is impossible. After the people dispersed and realized the futility of their aspirations, they reunited and achieved the degree of the Creator with the help of the forces of bestowal.

(Let me remind you that we're studying the roots, i.e., the Creator's forces. Everything that has ever taken place on the physical plane, on this earth, has its own Upper spiritual root. This is why the "Tower of Babel," which existed in the corporeal world, also exists in us.)

"The Creator put all the gathered earth atop Mount Moriah, where the sacrificial altar shall be in the Temple. He mixed it with water taken from all the oceans of the world, and from the resulting clay He fashioned the body of man."

Where was man created? He was created in a special place where the spiritual origin touches the corporeal one, at the point of contact between the two adjacent degrees. However, although we are speaking of two adjacent degrees, there is a great chasm between them. This contact means that precisely above "Mount Moriah," the *Sephirot* descend from the heavens and touch the earth.

The reality above "Mount Moriah" is called the spiritual reality, whereas all that exists below is called "the material world." The peak of Mount Moriah is a spiritual summit, the highest possible point in this world, where the Holy of Holies will be built. It towers over all the material of this world, and the greatest spiritual forces assemble there. It is precisely where man—the "coordinator" between the material and the spiritual dimensions—was created.

Both these worlds, the material and the spiritual, are present in Adam, and he can establish balance between them, using them as a single whole. In so doing, he elevates our entire reality to the spiritual level.

"Then the Lord God formed man from the dust of the ground, and breathed into his nostrils the breath of life; and man became a living soul." We mustn't forget that we're always talking about what's happening within. This is where "man" was just "born." You have undergone the phases of development of the still, vegetative, and animate desires, and now you're no longer fulfilled by all that pertains to them. Now you want another level—the spiritual one!

If you catch yourself thinking this way, it means the point in the heart has awakened within you and is drawing you to the Creator. If you don't want this incarnation going to waste, follow your point and listen to your inner voice. You are now "on the line" with the Upper One. You weren't born into the world to simply live your life and die. In fact, you're not supposed to die at all.

You are now exiting your corporeal ego, the lowest state: "Then the Lord God formed man of the dust of the ground." He let the "human" inside you feel the true and pure state, the quality of bestowal, life... (in the spiritual world, the ego stands for death, and bestowal stands for life) "...and breathed into his nostrils the breath of life."

You begin to identify with the point in the heart that is drawing you to the Creator. You enjoy being in this state, and you want to acquire spiritual sensations. This is the meaning of "...and man became a living soul." The human inside you has been born. If you follow this "human," He will surely lead you into the "land that flows with milk and honey," and there you will see the Creator.

What does it mean to "see the Creator"? He has many names, but the one that relates to us is *Boreh*. It consists of two words: *Bo* (come) and *Re'eh* (see). In other words, you will see the Creator; no one else can do it for you.

THE GARDEN OF EDEN

"And the Lord God planted a garden eastward, in Eden; and there He put the man whom He had formed."

What is a "garden?" It is man's qualities, which, utilized correctly, will provide him with the opportunity to reach the spiritual world. This "garden" (man's qualities) was "planted" for the sole purpose of leading us to the Goal. The garden is "planted" within us by the Creator, which means that we cannot attribute any of our qualities to ourselves.

Try to imagine that the people around you, the entire universe, are all your qualities projected into your consciousness. It only appears to us that something exists on the outside. In fact, as we correct ourselves, we begin to perceive that all of these are our own qualities, which exist within us. People, animals, plants, planets, the entire world, and the entire universe—everything exists within us.

The moment we attain this, we are left one-on-one with the Creator, and we understand that nothing exists but we and the Creator. (Don't worry if it seems confusing. As you continue to clarify the true meaning of the Eternal Book for yourself, these clarifications will allow you to increasingly develop this sensation.)

"And out of the ground made the Lord God to grow every tree that is pleasant to the sight and good for food; the tree of life also in the midst of the garden, and the tree of the knowledge of good and evil."

As you can see, no matter how we condemn or curse the ego, it is still our nature. Our desire is egoistic. In the Midrash on *Genesis* it grows from the ego, as it is said, "And God Almighty grew from the earth all manner of tree." (We are learning to understand the meaning of the book, and I am deliberately repeating myself to cement in your memory the terminology that will soon allow you to see the inner meaning of all the corporeal words and phrases.)

So what is the meaning of, "the tree of life also in the midst of the garden, and the tree of the knowledge of good and evil"? The "tree of life" is the higher part of your soul, the quality of bestowal that draws you. It is that innermost quality that's close to the Creator, which is why it is written to be "in the midst of the garden," at the center of all your qualities. The "tree of knowledge of good and evil" is the lower part of your soul, the quality of reception, your egoistic component.

Here is where the issue of good and evil comes into play. It depends on how you utilize your ego, and this is called the "intention." Will it be aimed at fulfilling yourself or fulfilling others? Destruction or creation? Let's see what happens next.

"And a river went out of Eden to water the garden." What is this river that flows out of Eden to water the garden? The "river" is the Upper Light, nourishing your quality of bestowal from within, imparting confidence that you can exist without desiring anything for yourself. How can you claim that you don't want anything for yourself? You can if you have the opportunity to possess everything. It is the sensation of security and serenity that is provided by the river (Upper Light) that waters everything. Nourishment from it enables all things to bear fruit.

And the Lord God took the man, and put him into the garden of Eden to dress it and to keep it. "And the Lord God commanded the man, saying: 'Of every tree of the garden you may freely eat; but of the tree of the knowledge of good and evil, you shall not eat of it; for in the day that you eat thereof you shall surely die.'"

You currently exist in an exalted state, for you have finally attained the "human" in you. He is Adam (we previously mentioned that Adam in Hebrew stems from the word *Domeh* (similar), meaning resembling the Creator). All your desires at this stage are in euphoria from attaining the spiritual world. You feel good in this Light, and you wish to continue living and breathing only in this way. This is the meaning of, "And the Lord God took the man, and put him into the garden of Eden to dress it and to keep it."

At this moment, it is as if you forget that inside you lurks the ego, that you're surrounded by egoistic, worldly desires for money, fame, power and knowledge. It is as if you say to the Creator, "I don't need any of this; I am happy simply being in Your Light."

Suddenly you hear the warning, "Of every tree of the garden you may freely eat; but of the tree of the knowledge of good and evil, you shall not eat of it; for in the day that you eat thereof you shall surely die."

Presently, you exist in this "garden" with your qualities of bestowal. They will never "harm" you because they are aimed at bestowing upon others. Therefore, "Of every tree of the garden you may freely eat."

However, if you use your egoistic qualities, "...but of the tree of the knowledge of good and evil, you shall not eat," the Light will instantly vanish and you will find yourself disconnected from the Creator, the universal Law of Life, from bestowal. It is precisely this state that is called death: "...for in the day that you eat thereof you shall surely die." Connecting to the Creator is life; disconnecting from Him is death.

This should be understood as explained below: When a "human" is born inside you, you mustn't rouse the full extent of your ego. Because you still cannot correct it, you mustn't use it. That is, the "human in you" must not eat from the tree of knowledge of good and evil, as that would harm him. Even though the fruits may seem big, ripe, and tasty, they are poisonous.

Thus lives the "human in you," the "human" desire or "Adam" in you, rejoicing in his bliss. The ego has not yet manifested in him in any way.

He is in the Garden of Eden, amidst the allowed pleasures, reveling in its serenity and in his closeness to the Creator.

But this is only for the time being. In Kabbalah, the state when egoistic desires are not utilized is called *Katnut* (infancy). It is when you consciously deny them, knowing that you're too weak and wouldn't be able to refrain from taking for yourself. The state of *Katnut* is described as putting a "screen" on the egoistic desires.

It is as if you say to yourself, "No, I will not receive! I won't be able to resist and instead will take for myself, and all will fall into my egoism. But I want to learn to bestow, like You. So what can I do? I have only one option: I won't receive anything. I don't want to take for myself. I want nothing! And so I'm erecting a screen on everything."

Again, a screen represents the strength of resistance against the ego. Of course, it works only as long as we can continue resisting, until a pleasure we cannot resist comes along. Then our resistance is broken and we take—and the screen breaks as we sink into the ego once more.

Our time has not yet arrived. It's only preparing to arrive...

MAN'S WIFE

"And the Lord God said: 'It is not good that the man should be alone; I will make him a help made against him.'"

Indeed, it is not good for man, who was created in God's image and likeness, to have only the Creator's power and nothing of man himself (meaning his egoistic nature). "It is not good that the man should be alone." That is, it is not good that he is stifled by the Light, and has no free will. Bit by bit, his nature must be awakened, his ego revealed to the extent that he can control it. Thus, his ego would stand "behind him." That is to say, the ego could be utilized, but would remain under his control.

The "woman in us" is the embodiment of this controlled ego.

"And the Lord God caused a deep sleep to fall upon the man (Adam), and he slept; and He took one of his ribs, and closed up the place with flesh instead thereof. And from the rib, which the Lord God had taken from the man, He made a woman and brought her unto the man. And the man said, 'This is now bone of my bones, and flesh of my flesh; she shall be called Woman because she was taken out of Man.'"

"Sleep" is a spiritual state, as if man dies, when all the types of Light leave him. In this uncontrolled state, a force awakens in him that he didn't want to use before. Man didn't want to activate his ego.

Why is that? He resides in the Creator's Garden of Eden and is completely under the authority of the Light. Man exists in a kind of narcotic state, but he must ultimately become free, for the Creator's objective was to make a creature equal to Him, rather than a slave to the Light. It follows that sooner or later, man must begin to activate his ego and correct it.

When the Light "exits him," when the "Adam" in him falls asleep, an "operation" can be performed: "He took one of his ribs, and closed up the place with flesh instead thereof. And the rib, which the Lord God had taken from the man, He made a woman, and brought her unto the man."

Naturally, this did not refer to a Adam's physical body. I hope that you, the reader, have gotten used to the fact that we're looking beyond the material images of these words for their true spiritual meaning. We're always speaking about desires, and nothing else!

A rib is a "place" in the chest where the altruistic desire in us connects to the egoistic desire.

In each of our desires is a vulnerable, but absolutely essential "place." It is the moment of doubt and struggle, when the temptation arises to take for yourself, even though you've already decided to "start a new life" and be exclusively in bestowal. This is the material from which "your inner woman" is made, and it exists in every one of us.

This material is that very common quality that exists between the desire to bestow and the desire to receive.

You may ask, "What could they possibly have in common?" The male desire within you strives to receive spiritual pleasure by bestowing upon others, upon the Creator. It waits for the moment when man declares, "I will take only the bare essentials for myself, and gladly bestow everything else to the Creator."

The female desire within you strives to receive spiritual pleasure, but for its own delight, realizing that this pleasure is the greatest in existence.

This common point is called "receiving pleasure," and the only difference is who you are fulfilling with this action: yourself or others.

If the desire to receive spiritual pleasure for self (female desire) is not controlled by the male desire to bestow, it becomes man's demise (in the spiritual sense).

Try to understand that what you see and feel is imaginary. In fact, besides you, there is only the Creator. "For the Creator's sake" and "for one's own sake" are the exact same thing. Until you reach the state of the end of correction, this illusion that others exist will persist. But then you will see that there are no "others"; there are only "me and the Creator."

But if the desire to bestow (male desire) submits to or follows the desire to receive for oneself (female desire), that will spell demise for man, as well.

Advancement can be infinite, as your soul has no limitation with respect to capacity, for through the soul you connect to others. The soul is the communicator with other souls. One can connect all of humanity to himself–to feel, think and understand in their stead. You need only "exit" yourself and "enter" them.

This is the essence of the Biblical principle, "Love your neighbor as yourself." What is our true egoism? It is when you love yourself egoistically, willing to disregard the whole world just to grab something for yourself. If you can exit yourself and give up all your possessions, you will begin to feel other people and become eternal. Therefore, there is no limit to your spiritual growth; we simply aren't taught this practice. Everyone can actualize himself and become equal to the Creator. Moreover, it is everyone's responsibility and duty to do so.

We will expound on this junction of the male and female beginnings in our desires later and clarify the necessary proportions. In the meantime, let us understand that their true coalescence lies in submission to the Light, in aspiring to it no matter what.

To summarize, the manifestation of an egoistic quality in Adam, which he had never felt before, is the birth of a "woman," the additional, external form called "Eve." Adam and Eve are the same flesh, in that they create between them a combination that has a right to exist independently. They support one another, whereas before they (the desire to bestow and the desire to receive) were estranged from one another.

"Therefore shall a man leave his father and his mother, and shall cleave unto his wife, and they shall be one flesh." Until that moment, all our desires depended on a single need: to remain in the Garden of Eden, to always be in the Creator's Light. This is how we feel when in the state of ascent, when we think only of spiritual pleasures, while everything else seems empty and worthless. This means that we are "in the Garden of Eden," connected to "our father and mother."

We do not lower our eyes to the "sinful earth," thinking that we've "departed" it and are now aspiring only upward. But earth cannot be escaped. Our nature is egoistic and must be corrected. The connection to the earth (desire to receive) is the "woman" to which "man" attaches, becoming one flesh with her, meaning drawing to himself egoistic desires, but not yet exposing them. Neither the man nor the woman have yet discovered themselves: "And they were both naked, the man and his wife, and were not ashamed."

The term "naked" alludes to the absence of "clothes"— that is, egoistic desires that coat man, clothes-like, concealing his true, primordial yearning for the spiritual world.

By donning these "clothes"—newer and newer egoistic desires—man distances himself from the Creator, although the spiritual basis always remains in him. He simply needs to begin to remove these layers and always strive for the root—the Creator who created us all. This is exactly what we are now doing.

If you're thinking of one thing and one thing only—how to equalize yourself with the Creator—you thus evoke a highly intense influence of the purifying Light. You are "bathing" yourself in true thoughts, with a true book, reading it the way Kabbalists do at supernal spiritual degrees. It is as if you've caught a lifeline that they threw to you. Now the important thing is to hold on!

"Naked" means a complete absence of egoistic intentions. This is why the Kabbalists weren't ashamed of their desires.

Likewise, animals don't need to conceal their actions; they are driven by instincts, not by egoistic desires. Man is the only creature that can blush with shame or needs to "cover" his intentions, for they are egoistic through and through.

But at this time, at the beginning of the path, the separated Adam and Eve (our desires) are naked and uncovered. They have nothing to be ashamed of because they lead a "beastly" existence, run by instincts. This is what living by instincts is called in our world.

They are naked and unashamed, for shame is the discovery of one's opposition to the Creator, which Adam and Eve have yet to realize.

THE SERPENT APPEARS

"Now the serpent was more subtle than any beast of the field which the Lord God had made. And he said unto the woman: 'Indeed, God has said, 'You shall not eat of any tree of the garden.'' And the woman said unto the serpent: 'Of the fruit of the trees of the garden we may eat; but of the fruit of the tree which is in the midst of the garden, God has said: 'You shall not eat of it, neither shall you touch it, lest you die.'' And the serpent said unto the woman: 'You shall not surely die; for God knows that in the day you eat thereof, your eyes shall open, and you shall be as God, knowing good and evil.'"

What exactly happened here? I trust that you, the reader, are beginning to "feel out" your thoughts and desires, and perceive this story differently, reading it with your inner vision.

Clearly, the "serpent" is your egoistic desire, your nature. (The "serpent" is the fourth and final phase of the ego.) Later, we will talk about how we cannot work with the serpent until we are strong enough to overcome this final phase of the ego, called *Lev HaEven* (the stony heart). It's with good reason that it's called "stony." Only the Creator can overcome it, and that is what happens once we complete our correction. The process is finalized by the Creator.

You may ask how the serpent ended up in the Garden of Eden? Well, if no one is using the serpent for evil purposes, he exists on the same level as everything else the Creator has made, in its true, primordial form as God's creation. If he doesn't use his desires for the sake of reception, his egoism is unrevealed, and in such a state he may be wherever he likes.

You would be right to ask, "What is the reason that the serpent (our ego) revealed itself?" Why didn't it just go on living in the Garden of Eden, without leading man to sin?

The answer is that man would then remain on the level of an angel, "infertile," while the goal is for him to become human! This is why the serpent (ego) reveals itself. It is precisely what man needs to rise from the level of the Garden of Eden to the Creator's level, and of his own volition.

Why, then, does the serpent go through Eve? Eve is that concealed ego that already exists in Adam (the desire to bestow). Eve is the bridge that links Adam to the real, powerful ego (man's nature, as ego can only be connected through ego). So when the time comes to execute this connection, the serpent appears before Eve: "And he said unto the woman: 'Indeed, God has said, 'You shall not eat of any tree of the garden.'"

Because Eve is the egoistic part of Adam (the quality of bestowal), she resists the serpent because she wishes to keep Adam pure, an angel, so she can stay with him in the Garden.

"And the woman said unto the serpent: 'Of the fruit of the trees of the garden we may eat; but of the fruit of the tree which is in the midst of the garden, God has said: 'You shall not eat of it, neither shall you touch it, lest you die.'"

However, according to the Creator's plan, Adam must become truly human, and grow from the state of *Katnut* (infancy) he is in, to the state of *Gadlut* (adulthood). He will achieve this after finally demonstrating his ego to the full extent, but using it exclusively to benefit others, for the sake of the Creator. This is why the true ego insists: "And the serpent said unto the woman: 'Ye shall not surely die; for God knows that in the day you eat thereof, your eyes shall open, and you shall be as God, knowing good and evil.'"

In other words, our "serpent" insists that this is the only way to actualize a true act of bestowal toward the Creator. That is, carrying out a true act of bestowal toward the Creator involves attaching the whole egoism, and achieving the goal of Creation, namely equivalence with the Creator, all in one go. (The serpent didn't lie. He was speaking from the end goal when this will happen one way or the other. He had only the best intentions.)

The Eve in man thinks that he really will be able to deal with his ego. He feels confident and doesn't doubt for a second that he will not stumble off the spiritual path.

This is how every beginner feels. Remember when you first discovered the spiritual truths? At that moment you were absolutely certain that from this point on you would aspire only toward the spiritual world, and will never again return to primitive corporeal desires. You thought you'd be able to "explain" to your ego all the advantages of the spiritual path.

Then, you suddenly became overburdened with tangible problems, like an opportunity to make lots of money, or a career promotion that required twelve hours of work daily. These material benefits gave you a momentary, but very tangible result, like money, respect, and possibilities for further growth, and you completely forgot that just yesterday you felt as if the Creator would reveal Himself to you any moment now, and place you in His "Garden of Eden." You forgot all about it and fell back into your corporeal desires. But the record of that blissful feeling of spiritual heights you experienced remains in you, and this is more important than anything else.

That is what the current chapter of the Pentateuch speaks of. It describes what happens when Eve (the egoistic desire that's not connected to the spiritual, to Adam) joins forces with the serpent (the primordial, earthly egoism) and heeds his words: "And when the woman saw that the tree was good for food, and that it was a delight to the eyes, and that the tree was to be desired to make one wise..."

In other words, you thought this action would bring you to the goal, that it was "good for food," just as the serpent claimed.

That is when the strongest egoistic desire enters you—your Adam, your most ardent desire to attain the spiritual state. This causes the "breaking of your Adam," the pure spiritual desire, and this is "the fall of man" (Adam).

"...she took from its fruit and ate; and she gave also to her husband with her, and he ate." You were certain you'd prevail, that you would do it for the sake of advancing spiritually. That was your sincere intention. The Adam in you "eats," meaning attaches to himself egoism he has never used before. Naturally, he did not prevail; he began to use the pleasure for himself. "The eyes of them both were opened, and they knew that they were naked."

Indeed, they discovered the Light of Love, the Creator's Light that surrounded them all that time. "And the eyes of them both were opened," but then they also saw each other in that Light, and realized that they were absolutely opposite to Him. The Light (Creator) is pure, absolute bestowal, whereas they are thoroughly egoistic ("and they knew that they were naked").

They understood that they were egoists and couldn't be like Him, having felt their corruption, their disparity from the Creator on the one hand, and their individuality, uniqueness and ability to achieve correction on the other hand. You could say this was the first manifestation of man's "I." Until that moment, he existed in the general Light, fully devout to the Creator, when suddenly his "eyes were opened": There is my "I," there is my ego. If only he knew the full breadth of the ascents and descents that this great discovery would bring to every individual and all of humanity in the future!

THE EXILE

What follows is only the exile and nothing else, all the way down to our world. "By the sweat of your face you will eat bread, till you return to the ground, because from it you were taken; for you are dust, and to dust you shall return."

What was the reason for the exile? Why did the Creator conceive and execute this "operation" of breaking an exalted spiritual desire into many pieces, which fell into our world and clothed themselves in bodies? They forgot all about the fairytale garden and don't perceive the spiritual world whatsoever. They feel no influence of the spiritual Light, but are occupied with themselves, catering to their petty corporeal desires, clashing their egos in wars, discord, and hatred. Indeed, what was the reason for breaking this great, unified soul of Adam?

The breaking allowed the most important thing to happen: the sparks of bestowal, the altruistic desires of Man (Adam) fell into the kingdom of egoism and saturated it with the "spirit of bestowal." A "recording" was made in our egoism that there is such a great thing as a spiritual connection with the Creator, which is unbelievable joy that's difficult to express in words.

It is precisely this feeling that will come into play later. It will remain dormant in our egos, waiting for an opportunity that will certainly come, for everything develops exclusively by the Creator's design. Then, these sparks of spiritual experience, latent and biding their time, will illuminate the kingdom of egoism, and a path will appear in the total darkness. Like a seeing man leading the blind on a path, so will these sparks lead the egoistic desires toward the Light, toward correction.

That time has come. Humanity realizes it has reached a dead end, that it cannot progress to a good life. We already feel the harm inherent in egoism, and we blame it for all the deadly sins: "...for you are dust, and to dust you shall return." We perceive it as dust from which nothing grows but war, depression, terrorism, and an endless string of suffering. This sensation signifies that the Creator is calling us to Him. He has "shone" His Light on us, and in it we saw ourselves as we really are—a sight so terrifying that we began to seek a way out of our selves. This is called "a prayer."

It is precisely in this situation that the sparks of the soul of the first man awaken in us. They exist in everyone. Soon we will all feel them and realize we are parts of the one soul, one organism, and we'll wish to return "Home," living in unity with all the other souls, for without it we won't survive.

"Therefore the Lord God sent him forth from the garden of Eden, to till the ground from whence he was taken. So He drove out the man; and He placed at the east of the garden of Eden the cherubim, and the flaming sword which turned every way, to keep the way to the tree of life."

So, this is the Creator's plan. Obviously, the act of the breaking was preordained. Otherwise, the "kingdom of darkness" would reign within us forever, and we would never awaken to feel the spiritual world as we crawl on the ground and consume dust like serpents. (Incidentally, this is exactly why our primordial, uncorrected egoism is called "a serpent," because our desire to receive crawls on the ground.)

The serpent cannot rise above this desire (it has no arms or legs; it is bound to the ground and cursed by the Creator, which means it is opposite from Him, and all this brings man only suffering).

"Because you have done this, cursed are you more than all cattle, and more than every beast of the field; on your belly you will go, and dust you will eat all the days of your life." This is how we perceive our egoism.

Of course, there aren't any curses from the Creator's side. He never changes; He is the absolute good, and always remains the same—in total bestowal. Only we change. Today, more than ever, we recognize that our nature is opposite from the Creator's, and that egoism has led us to a dead end.

Indeed, it is the Creator who has brought us to this state of futility, for there is no other force in the world—no demons, no devils, no witches—there is only the Creator. To compel us to independently ascend to His level, He has placed us in this situation.

Moreover, on our way back to Him we will need to undergo trials: "He placed at the east of the garden of Eden the cherubim, and the flaming sword which turned every way, to keep the way to the tree of life." These trials are prepared for our benefit, for by overcoming them we form a single desire—to return to our previous state of our own volition, and live in accordance with the law of unity and love. Only then will the angels with swords allow us to enter the garden, and we won't need to return to the suffering of this world. Instead we will attain the Creator's secrets in infinite delight.

Now let us take a brief pause to clarify the text, and try to understand the whole picture. This will simplify our journey onward.

ON FREE WILL

From the above we've learned that one gradually learns to sense this world and the Upper World, and their interaction at the same time. Information descends from the Upper World into ours and manifests as matter. We see physical objects, plants, animals, birds, insects, and people. But if we possess spiritual vision in addition to the corporeal one, we can also sense the forces that govern matter.

It is precisely this perception of reality that everyone must achieve: to sense the Creator behind everything that exists and transpires. We needn't believe it blindly, but actually see and sense it. This is what the book teaches us.

Our reaction to the forces that descend from above as information ascends to the Upper World, where our future is decided, whether it materializes in a good result or a bad one.

Being at the highest spiritual degree, the Creator created the creature from the quality of egoism, which is opposite to Him. He filled the creature with the Light, and then emptied it, thereby lowering it to the state called "our world."

In return, the creature ascends back along the spiritual degrees, thereby meriting pleasures far greater than what it had before its descent into this world.

A question arises: to reach equivalence with its Maker, why did the creature need to experience the worst possible state? Couldn't it be avoided?

The fact is that the creature must have the strength and freedom to act freely in between two opposite qualities: its own ego and the Creator, to freely choose its own path and independently follow it.

To provide man with these choices means the Creator must a) completely distance the creature from Himself, b) give the creature the ability to develop and attain the Universe, and c) allow the creature freedom of choice.

The Creator provides the creature with these conditions gradually. The creature that senses the Creator, and is therefore filled with the Light, is not autonomous. Rather, it is fully controlled by the Light, which dictates its own terms and imparts to it its qualities.

To create a fully autonomous and independent creature, the Creator must distance Himself from it completely. In other words, by freeing itself from the Light, the creature achieves independence in its actions. The act whereby the Light is extracted is called *Tzimtzum* (restriction).

Imagine having a flawed tool that you need to work with. Naturally, the first thing you must do is fix it and make it serviceable before you can use it.

From the very first pages, this is exactly what the Bible speaks of: how to repair this unusable tool—our soul—and return to the Creator as a result. Like an instruction manual, it explains how one can ascend to the most supernal and perfect state, while still living in this world.

As was already mentioned, during the correction one exists between two worlds—the Upper and the lower. In the process of correction the soul acquires the necessary skills, knowledge, and experience for the correction. More importantly, one develops new sensations, new spiritual qualities. Thus, by achieving complete correction of the soul, one acquires the qualities that allow for existence in all the Upper Worlds—in eternity, serenity, and perfection. This is how we come to the end of correction.

This state is not described anywhere for the simple reason that it cannot be expressed in words. Only those who go through all the preliminary states and reach the end of correction attain it. Beyond the end of correction lie uncharted territories that hold the so-called "secrets of the Torah" (*Maase Merkava* and *Maase Beresheet*).

There are only isolated hints at them in *The Book of Zohar* and other Kabbalistic texts. However, those spiritual spheres cannot be described because our language, our letters, and our notions are all taken from the world of correction.

We cannot sense anything that exists above the system of correction. Therefore, we cannot express them in our human language, which is confined to our coordinates, notions and perceptions.

This is why the greatest Kabbalist of the modern age, Baal HaSulam, pleaded with the Creator to allow him to descend from the world of true perceptions to a lower degree, so he could communicate the way to the spiritual dimension using letters, words, and earthly emotions. When his request was granted, he penned the main Kabbalistic works for our generation, which we can use to enter the spiritual realm. His works are like a map without which you will surely lose your way in the labyrinth of corporeal life, lose hope, grow weary and pass away without ever learning the true purpose of your existence. Like a father responding to the suffering of his children, Baal HaSulam picks us up and carries us to the Light.

Just as one cannot exist in our world without understanding it, the soul cannot exist in the spiritual world after the body passes without acquiring knowledge about it beforehand. Therefore, all the achievements in the science of Kabbalah not only guarantee us a comfortable existence in this world, but also the opportunity to exist in the world to come.

BACK TO ADAM

Let us now return to the First Man, to Adam, that desire which we feel within. When the Creator exiled him from the Garden of Eden, the "human in us" (Adam) stopped being a child and began to mature.

The maturation process is a period when we know we must correct our egoism, for we cannot live with it or to simply suppress it.

There is no immediate correction, as the "serpent" suggested. Instead, man must descend all the way down until he feels the full span of his ego and begs the Creator for help, realizing that he's powerless to deal with it on his own.

"And the man knew Eve his wife; and she conceived and bore Cain, and said: 'I have gotten a man with the help of the Lord.' And again she bore his brother Abel. And Abel was a keeper of sheep, but Cain was a tiller of the ground."

This is the beginning of the descent. We see how a great egoistic desire that man could not deal with began to split into pieces. (There is a breaking whereby sparks fly into our world, where they receive egoistic shells—bodies. I will reiterate here that we're talking about our work with the egoistic desires exclusively, and not about specific people.)

"And the man knew Eve his wife." This means the altruistic and egoistic desires merged in man. The result was a merging, or "giving birth," to two desires: Cain and Abel.

One desire, Abel, gravitates toward bestowal, toward the Creator. This is why it is written that he doesn't till the ground, but "keeps sheep." He can be the "guide" and lead the way to fertile pastures. Whom does he lead there? Man's egoistic desires, which are ready to follow him, foretasting the future pleasures. It is precisely these desires that are called "sheep."

The desire called "Abel" is also called the "right line." The right line is an altruistic desire, an aspiration for the Creator without a trace of egoism. This desire is sent down to us from above, like an outstretched hand or a lowered ladder that we can climb to the Goal.

The desire called "Cain" is the left line. This is the exact opposite—an egoistic desire and an aspiration to use the bond with the Creator for one's own fulfillment.

In the story about Cain and Abel, the distancing from the Creator is not yet complete. That is, there is no situation such as in our world, where the Creator is absolutely concealed, the mind contends that it's all a sham, and that man ought to live only for himself.

Here we have a different picture. We are in a dialogue with the Creator: He is felt and the spiritual world is near, but the desires are different.

Abel has pure desires, the desire to bestow, to receive pleasure from delighting the Creator. It would appear that Cain also has the desire to bestow, but in his case he strives to win the Creator's favor, to merit His attention, to acquire the spiritual world. He wants to receive all the Light and the infinite pleasure it contains, but only for himself.

Cain represents the left line, which "tills the ground." This means that our desire named Cain is always working with the ego. If Cain doesn't master the ego, the ego masters Cain. That is what's referred to in the following passage: "And in the process of time it came to pass that Cain brought of the fruit of the ground an offering unto the Lord. And Abel also brought of the firstlings of his flock and of the fat thereof. And the Lord had respect unto Abel and to his offering; but unto Cain and to his offering He had no respect. And Cain was very wroth, and his countenance fell. And the Lord said unto Cain: 'Why are you wroth? and why is your countenance fallen? If you do well, shall it not be lifted up? and if you do not do well, sin crouches at the door; and unto you is its desire, but you may rule over it.'"

"...but you may rule over it," such is the call of Nature. You must work on your egoistic desires, rather than suppress or try to eliminate them because not receiving isn't an option for you. This is how you were created. You are required to ascend above them, to use them, to *master* your egoistic desires, i.e., to receive pleasure from delighting the Creator.

That is the state at which man must ultimately arrive. Therein lies the purpose of man's creation. Otherwise his ego will rule over him, and the result of its reign will be all the things humanity is afflicted with today: war, death, and tragedies.

That is what became of Cain.

"And Cain spoke unto Abel his brother. And it came to pass, when they were in the field, that Cain rose up against Abel his brother, and slew him."

What does the fratricide mean here? It means that the left line suppresses the right. In other words, the egoistic line asserts the following, "I'm the only one that's useful around here; I act, I harvest, I till the land, and I should be the one to be rewarded for all this."

Makes sense, doesn't it? Sure, but it is this sensible approach that "kills" the right line, which claims that the only way is pure bestowal and absolute equivalence with the Creator. Here, the only permissible state is to delight Him without any concern of reward.

So what is the Creator's verdict?

"When you till the ground, it shall not henceforth yield unto you her strength; a fugitive and a wanderer shall you be in the earth."

The strength of the earth, the desire, lies precisely in the combination of the right and left lines, in finding "the golden mean," where man delights in reception only when he thus bestows upon another. This is the only way we can remain in infinite bliss.

But if this combination doesn't take place, i.e., if "Abel is killed," the earth cannot yield strength, but actually drains it, as all the efforts you made become labor for your own ego, for the left line, for Cain. The ego can never be satiated. This is why it is written, "a fugitive and a wanderer shall you be in the earth," that is, you will be trying to find happiness in vain.

"Behold, You have driven me out this day from the face of the land; and from Your face shall I hide; and I shall be a fugitive and a wanderer in the earth; and it will come to pass, that whosoever finds me will slay me."

As already mentioned, killing or suppressing the ego is impossible. It lives forever, growing, passing from generation to generation, and losing touch with the Creator all the while.

It is therefore written: "And the Lord said unto him: 'Therefore whosoever slays Cain, vengeance shall be taken on him sevenfold.' And the Lord set a sign for Cain, lest any finding him should smite him."

This moment marks the beginning of the story of humankind, the process in which your soul descends from the Creator to our world. The soul itself does not change throughout the process, but simply dons egoistic garments that conceal it, dampening its voice, its eternal bond with the Creator. Thus it transforms from the single, unified heart of Adam into myriad points of an infinite number of people.

The Creator always remains connected to the soul in the part we call the "point in the heart." This is why there ultimately comes a time when you "hear" His voice once more, sensing a feeble luminescence bursting through the filters and barriers. That's when you begin to aspire to return to the spiritual world, to the Creator, longing for the Garden of Eden.

"And Cain knew his wife; and she conceived, and bore Enoch; and he built a city, and called the name of the city after the name of his son Enoch. And unto Enoch was born Irad; and Irad begot Mehujael; and Mehujael begot Methushael; and Methushael begot Lamech."

And so on, and so forth... Humanity begins to procreate, its numbers are growing, but you already know that all these "people" are really your egoistic desires. It is your mission to correct them, whereupon you will return once more to the one soul of Adam, having joined with it into a single whole.

THE SECRETS OF THE ETERNAL BOOK

So why was the great egoistic desire (the serpent and Cain) shattered into myriad tiny, egoistic desires? It happened because it's easier to correct myriad tiny desires than one great desire. By correcting them, we reassemble the one great desire and restore the one soul in the Garden of Eden.

There is an old parable of a king who wished to send a great fortune to his son in another kingdom. This presented the king with a dilemma: he knew his people were all thieves and there wasn't anyone in the whole kingdom he could trust with so much wealth.

So after giving the matter some thought, he found a way. The king exchanged all of his fortune into coins of minor value, dispersed them among his subjects, and tasked them with delivering them to his son in the neighboring kingdom. Naturally, the people couldn't be bothered with pocketing such a small sum; it was more important to showcase their loyalty and obedience to the king. Every one of them fulfilled his duty with honor, and the entire fortune reached its destination.

Reflect on this story; it holds a great deal of meaning, which could help you draw the right conclusion from all we discussed in this chapter.

CHAPTER 2

NOAH

"Noah was in his generations a man righteous and whole-hearted; Noah walked with God." So begins the chapter on Noah, immediately confusing the reader with what appears to be a straightforward story about our world.

However, it confuses only those who aren't yet ready to read the Bible differently, still finding the simple historical narrative about a person named Noah satisfactory.

Let us leave them to their search for Noah's Ark on Mount Ararat, and delve into the text, instead. As much as we can, let us understand how it is connected to each and every one of us, to our spiritual search, to our souls, and the very purpose of our lives.

Let us start by recounting the topic of this chapter. Having seen that the earth is full of sin, God makes a covenant with Noah to build an ark and take shelter there with his wife, kids, and animals. In the meantime, God will flood the earth, effectively destroying everyone.

Then, Noah is to emerge from his ark with his family and the saved animals, and they will become the progenitors of future generations of people and animals on Earth. The people will wish to build a Tower of Babel and speak the same language, but they will fail. Then, they will disperse throughout the world and stop understanding one another.

Ask yourself, "Where am I in this story of Noah?" Or better yet, "What is the meaning of my inner Noah?" You must seek only one approach to the contents of this book: "Everything I read here is about me." Noah, the righteous, his wife, kids, and all the animals, the ark and the Tower of Babel all exist within me. They are forces, desires that govern my inner and outer worlds. All I have to do is get to them and sense them, and the gates to all the secrets will open for me.

In the previous chapter, *Beresheet* (Genesis, "In the Beginning") we spoke of the creation of the world, the abode of souls. We clarified how, following all the animal desires, the human desire was born, symbolizing man's aspiration for the spiritual world, for the Creator, which then shattered into myriad tiny pieces that fell into our world.

This descent is still continuing. It will continue until we are ready to face our primordial egos, to see our true "I." We have yet to arrive at this point; we must still be prepped to not only see the ego but endure it, and not only endure it, but resolve to escape from it.

Jumping a bit ahead, know that our "I" will be personified by Pharaoh. But we'll talk more about that later on. In the meantime, we're making our way to Pharaoh, to the complete realization that we are slaves to our egos. The descent has only just begun. For the moment, we feel as if we're still close to the spiritual world. We continue to sense the Light—this initial joy from meeting the Creator. In other words, the Creator isn't yet completely concealed from us, so the night of our escape from Egypt hasn't yet arrived.

However, we already feel ourselves as egoists, and this feeling is extremely distressing.

NOAH'S SPARK

"And God saw the earth, and, behold, it was corrupt; for all flesh had corrupted their way upon the earth." This means that all our desires are egoistic.

However, we still see amidst all that corruption a certain point, miniscule and lonely, which is completely opposite from everything else on the earth. This is the "point in the heart."

At the first egoistic level, this point is called "Noah." The Noah within us is our first spiritual desire. It may be tiny and barely discernible, but we already feel it living inside us. Thus, we have discovered Noah.

Noah's spark lives inside every one of us. The problem is that we've surrounded it with heaps of selfishness that continually drown out its soft voice. As the ego grew, it coated Noah with more and more layers, overwhelming it with incessant desires. The pursuit of pleasure distanced man from Noah, making him coarser and more egoistic as Noah's voice grew more and more faint. Finally, he has become essentially silent.

But Noah didn't go anywhere. He constitutes the basis of man's soul. Indeed, he is eternal, and simply waits for the time when man will turn back toward him.

In fact, this point we call "Noah" is the very center of our desires and is directly connected to the Creator. It is also eternal, whereas the egoistic desires surrounding it are short-lived, fleeting, vain and empty. Only that which aspires upward to the spiritual world is eternal, and that is where our desire known as "Noah" aims.

Dear reader, have you ever wanted to suddenly stop this crazy rat race we call "life," shut your eyes, cover your ears, and feel the silence that lives inside of you? Have you ever wished to hear the inner voice, un-obscured by foreign influences? Have you ever wished to hear your own voice, and in so doing, seemingly disappear from this world, which imposes on you its desires from dawn to dusk?

The TV, radio, and newspapers spray you with their advertisements; people both familiar and strangers force their thoughts and desires on you. Money! Power! Fame! That's what you hear left and right from your environment, until you start to think that these are actually your thoughts. Caught in the daily vortex of life, you can no longer tell whether it's you who wants these things or someone else.

Your inner voice has been suppressed, smothered by all that's happening around you. As you run along the highway of life, you're spurred on by foreign desires. It's only later that you realize that you were wrong, that you never wanted any of these things, that they were simply dictated to you, forced onto you by someone else.

How blissful it feels to be able to stop and hear your own, single desire, pure and disconnected from the material world. It's the desire to experience spirituality, which is known in the Old Testament as "Noah." It lives on inside of you, whether you're a president or a mass murderer. When you wade your way through the husk of foreign feelings and thoughts, you will ultimately arrive at Noah and hear the voice: "...for you have I seen righteous before Me in this generation."

If you can hear the Noah within you, this tiny altruistic spark called, "Noah the Righteous," if you can sense the desire to ascend above this world, then you are ready to achieve the peace, security, and eternity that await you on your spiritual path.

And if you're not, you will continue to spend every waking moment slaving away to foreign bodily desires, as they continue to whisper in your ear, "Go on, indulge in the pleasures of this world, live for yourself, don't be an idiot!"

And what happens when you succumb to these desires? The body grows feeble and dies and gets tossed into the ground to decompose. The death of the flesh is inevitable. A pity, isn't it? You work your entire life for the body, but in the end, it betrays you.

What about Noah? Well, Noah doesn't betray you because Noah is the desire of the eternal soul. It is connected to eternity, and if you attach yourself to Noah, you become eternal as well. It's that simple. All you have to do is to want it. That is precisely what the book speaks of in the chapter about Noah.

"And the earth was filled with violence... it was corrupt; for all flesh had corrupted their way upon the earth."

We remember that the word "earth" (Heb. *Eretz*) stems from the word *Ratzon*—desire. Therefore, "The earth was filled with violence" and "It was corrupt" means that your desires are corrupted: you exhaust yourself in pursuit of another's possessions, you are completely egoistic, and you live only for yourself. You already feel that this attitude causes destruction within and all around you (just look at what's happening in the world—we are tearing it to shreds with our egos).

But is there really no answer to all this? Sure there is. Find the "Noah" inside you and save your life, as the text says: "And, behold, I will destroy them with the earth." Follow the Creator's advice, as He is the Supernal Intellect or Supernal Law, and this is what He says: "But I will establish My covenant with you; and you shall come into the ark, you, and your sons, and your wife, and your sons' wives with you. And of every living thing of all flesh, two of every sort shall you bring into the ark, to keep them alive with you; they shall be male and female. Of the fowl after their kind, and of the cattle after their kind, of every creeping thing of the ground after its kind, two of every sort shall come unto you, to keep them alive."

What does this mean? The whole world is inside you. You are at the highest degree of existence, the tip of the pyramid that includes all the animate, vegetative, and inanimate souls located below you. They are "bound" to you as the one true creature that has a soul and the responsibility to raise itself and the whole world to the level of the Creator.

Thus, this chapter describes how the desire called "Noah" inside you assembles all the corrected parts of the soul (human, animate, vegetative and even the uncorrected parts that aspire for correction), which is the meaning of "two of every sort," and comes into the ark with them.

The ark is a kind of screen, a protective force field that you create around you, and that helps you resist external disturbances, meaning all the egoistic influences of this world.

You simply refuse to allow anything to enter you, negating all contact with your environment. By doing so, you don't become a hermit or abandon your family and this world altogether, absolutely not! You still go to work, make your living and go about your business as usual, but only externally. Internally, you try with all your might to deny entrance to the material world. With the help of the ark, the protective screen, you seek answers to the questions, "Who am I? What am I living for? What is most important to me in life?"

You haven't found the answer yet, but you keep searching, and that is already incredibly significant. You are preparing yourself to find the answer, and you are already certain that your search will be successful, since the point in the heart within you has already awakened and won't let you rest for a moment. This point maintains direct contact with the Creator, and as it grows within you, it forms a vessel that's ready to receive the Upper Light. That is the voice you hear, telling you you're on the right track and that you will definitely reach the Creator, even if you don't yet feel Him.

ENTERING THE ARK

Your entrance into the ark begins the moment you "sort out" your desires and select those with which you can continue to develop spiritually. Accordingly, you will understand which desires must be "drowned."

How is this done? We can do it primarily with the help of the books. In addition to this book, you seek out others like it, written by those who have already attained their root, the Upper World, and convey through them their attainment. These books are like roadmaps designed to guide you to your Goal via the shortest possible route. These books are few in number. They aren't meant to expand your knowledge, but to cultivate within you the sensation of the Upper One. They are written by great Kabbalists: Abraham, Moses, RASHBI (Rabbi Shimon Bar Yochai), the ARI, and Baal HaSulam. We will get back to these names later on.

So, if you refuse to let up until you've found the right books, it means you're "building an ark." You delve into the books, and at first, you don't understand them one bit, but you continue to read. This is how you "erect the walls of the ark."

Then, you find a teacher, a guide who will not let you stray from the path, and you find friends with whom you will overcome the obstacles that stand between you and the goal. This is how you "lay the roof of the ark."

And now you're inside the ark. In other words, you live in the material world, but under the right conditions. This is "your ark."

DIFFICULT QUESTIONS

"And I, behold, I do bring the flood of waters upon the earth, to destroy all flesh, wherein is the breath of life, from under heaven; every thing that is in the earth shall perish. But I will establish My covenant with you; and you shall come into the ark."

There it is again: "coming into the ark." Coming into the ark and escaping the flood is possible only if you switch off your mind, as odd as that may sound. "Switching off your mind" means you ignore the advice of the body, your ego. It's a difficult condition, but it can be done, and many have already traversed this journey. They wrote the authentic books about discovering the true, exalted force of love, which they called "the Creator." They also wrote that the tiniest grain of spiritual pleasure is billions of times greater than all of the earthly pleasures combined.

So, achieving the spiritual pleasure is possible only if you escape from the iron grip of the ego and conquer your mind. Of course, your mind bombards you with questions such as, "What are you doing this for?" and "What are you really getting out of it?" "Where are the tangible benefits?" "Who are these sages that you follow their instructions so closely?"

You hear all this, but your response to your mind is, "I understand your concerns but I have faith in the sages and in what I read in these books. I have faith in the path I'm on because without faith you cannot achieve anything in the spiritual world."

You respond to each objection your body raises in the same way: "Everything that's happening to me is the Upper Force's mercy, leading me to salvation. This mercy is indeed concealed, but I am walking toward it *despite* my mind. I will not stray from the path." This is the only answer that will bring you to the goal, and that is exactly the state called "entering the ark."

I realize that I have confused you, dear reader, that your mind is rebelling against such oppression, screaming, "Don't listen! You are an independent human being, capable of making independent decisions!"

Let me tell you a secret. Do you know who's feeding you these questions? It is the so-called "impure force," a.k.a., "the devil." This force has power only over your mind. But if you act in spite of your mind, you will immediately feel the kind of relief that comes after exhausting labor, because the power of the "pure force" means to do something in spite of the mind.

Now, this next notion may seem odd or bewildering, but you need to know that both the pure and the impure forces stem from the same source. That source is the Creator, a force of absolute good that wants one thing and one thing only: to turn us into creatures worthy of Him. It is He who confuses us, deliberately, so we can decide our fate for ourselves. Every decision, every step we take we will need to weigh carefully, as though our entire life hangs in the balance.

"And the flood was forty days upon the earth; and the waters increased, and bore up the ark, and it was lifted up above the earth. And the waters prevailed and increased greatly upon the earth; and the ark went upon the face of the waters. ...And all flesh perished that moved upon the earth... and Noah only was left, and they that were with him in the ark."

What is the meaning of, "the flood was forty days upon the earth"? It means the "earth"—your desire—is being "flooded with flood waters." "Flood waters" are the questions that literally "wash over" you.

As we mentioned earlier, these questions aren't simple. They are your mind's questions. They are materialistic, rational, pragmatic, and are triggered by problems that concern the body. In these questions ("flood waters") lurk the "angel of death." Their "where's" and "why's" aim to drown us.

Yes, the body becomes the "angel of death" when you begin your path toward spiritual ascension. The questions never let up; they return a thousand times: "What do you need this for? What's the point? Think about yourself because your efforts aren't bringing you any personal benefit. What will you get out of all this work? How will the Creator repay you for observing His commandments? Will it be worth it after all your toiling is done?"

These objections of the body are summed up by the question "What?" (Heb. Ma?)

If you oppose the body, citing faith in the Creator that He governs all things in the name of good, then the body objects even more. Now it screams, "Who?" (Heb. Mi) "Who is the Creator, that I should obey His voice?" If you only knew, if you could see and feel that the Creator is great, you could work for Him. Just consider how much more profitable it is to work for someone respected in our world.

It is when these two objections of the body combine in you that the two questions "What?" and "Who?" (Ma and Mi) merge into one word—Maim, which means "water" in Hebrew. And much Maim (water) creates a flood.

THE FLOOD

Maim is the flood that will drown your spiritual embryo if you heed the body's questions, destroying all that you've worked so hard to assemble within. Don't listen to it!

The flood comes as a ruthless force that can destroy everything. Those desires that couldn't endure the questions, meaning those that didn't "come into the ark," truly perish in its waters: "And all flesh perished that moved upon the earth." And yet, the paradox is that for all its ruthlessness, the flood also purifies.

However, it purifies only those in whom the desires to attain the spiritual world prevail. It is as if man doesn't even hear the rational questions of his body as he advances toward the goal, no matter what. In this case he acts like Noah, building himself an ark (finding the right books, the right teacher, and the right environment). He will also take shelter there with his numerous individual desires that are yet to be corrected (but will be corrected as the ark "sails" the flood waters).

"Then the flood came upon the earth for forty days, and the water increased and lifted up the ark, so that it rose above the earth." What is the meaning of these 40 days, during which your body pelted you with all your desires with its seemingly logical questions: "Ma?" and "Mi?"

Forty is a very significant number in spirituality. Naturally, we're not talking about days here. The number forty represents the quality of bestowal, the Creator's quality.

Forty is also the numerical value of the letter *Mem*. In Hebrew it is written as ם. As you can see, it resembles a closed space, but in reality it consists of two letters *Dalet* (ד) joined together. One of the two is upright (stemming from the Hebrew word *Delet*—door), while the other *Dalet* is upside down. When joined together they form a closed letter *Mem* (ם). However, when the moment comes, they will open.

If you manage to withstand those forty days of the mind's onslaught and not break, "the water will lift up the ark" and it will "float on the surface of the water." This means that the two letters *Dalet* lock and form a "sealed" letter *Mem*, and you "float."

You become a spiritual embryo in the womb of the mother (the Upper One, the closed *Mem*), which protects you, cares for you and feeds you. You remain under its full protection for as long as you grow there. Your Upper mother (Heb. *Ima*) won't let anything hurt you. You begin to float on the water, toward the Upper World.

"...and only Noah was left, together with those that were with him in the ark." Thus "water" transforms from a destructive force into the light of mercy for you, cleansing you and helping you advance. You ascend above the flood waters in which our world is currently drowning, torn apart by the ego and succumbing to the questions of the body.

Now let's repeat one last time how you can cleanse, rather than drown, in the time of the flood, and how you can become a "spiritual embryo" and enter the *Mem*. To accomplish this, you must pick up the necessary books and begin to "wash" yourself with them, as though with clean water. Bathe in the Light of Mercy, which, through your correct study, will cleanse you on the outside. You draw it like a magnet by reading these books, and it will fill you on the inside when you are open to the Light and its quality of bestowal, whereupon the Light will enter you.

It is precisely the Light of mercy that helps you reveal the one desire amidst all your other desires, the desire called Noah.

Like flood waters, the same Light "floods" those desires and forces within you that need to be "thoroughly drenched" so as to cleanse them for subsequent use.

How long must your desires for spiritual advancement remain in the ark? For as long as it takes for the "flood waters" to rise above the "earth" (your remaining desires) until they "drown" in the Light of Mercy, cleansing to such an extent that you can use them correctly for your inner, personal and only desire, known as "Noah."

"...The water decreased steadily until the tenth month; in the tenth month, on the first day of the month, the tops of the mountains became visible."

You were in the ark, detached from all the egoistic desires. You didn't use them, but remained "inside" the books and the thoughts of spiritual ascent, like an embryo in the mother's womb. You were under the Creator's protection, sheltered by Him. You reveled in that silence; it was like Paradise. But now you're grown and mature, and the time of your emergence into the world is nearing. It's time to begin your "exit from the ark."

Until now, you were constantly praying for your birth, which is called "raising MAN" to the Creator, the Upper One. The acronym MAN stands for *Mayin Nukvin* (female waters, referring to the amniotic fluid).

This means that you must begin your own path, to "leave the Creator's womb," as if with female waters, to be born and start working with your thus far "light" egoistic desires. You didn't take them with you into the "ark," having put them on hold for the right time. Now that they've been properly washed and cleansed with "flood waters," it's time for you to start correcting them.

In doing so you become increasingly closer to the spiritual world, to the Creator, since the end goal is the correction of the entire ego. Only then will you feel free, immortal, and absolutely blissful. This is what the Creator wants for you. This is the only condition under which you can be close to Him.

You have already begun traversing this path. Now don't stop!

So, the "waters break," much like amniotic fluid during labor.

BIRTH

"And the waters decreased continually until the tenth month." And then the "earth appears," meaning you draw to yourself the first egoistic desires, the lightest and most superficial, which are mountains. "In the tenth month, on the first day of the month, were the tops of the mountains are seen."

(Here they are, after the nine months of intrauterine development, with the embryo's birth on the first day of the tenth month.)

"And it came to pass at the end of forty days, that Noah opened the window of the ark which he had made. And he sent forth a raven, and it went forth to and fro, until the waters were dried up from off the earth. And he sent forth a dove... But the dove found no rest for the sole of her foot, and she returned unto him to the ark."

What's happening here? Think back to what you did the moment you were disconnected from the material world, having returned to it afterward with a specific program of correction. You took the light egoistic desires, known as "raven" and "dove," which were corrected in the ark, and used them to "feel the earth" (the desire). In so doing, you seemingly asked yourself, "Will the ego suck me in again?"

Why does this happen at the end of forty days, and what is the "window" that is made? Forty is the quality of the Creator, the quality of absolute bestowal, the quality of a mother. What you are doing here is making a "tiny window" in it. You are introducing a certain dissonance into this idyll by adding a dash of egoism to it. This enables you to check whether you can establish contact between your altruistic and egoistic qualities (by sending forth a raven and then a dove—qualities that have undergone correction in the ark). Can there be contact between the two? Can you "disembark," or not quite yet?

As it turns out, the answer is "no," since both birds return to the ark.

"And he stayed yet other seven days; and sent forth the dove." What are these seven days?

In Kabbalah, the number seven (7) symbolizes a small but complete desire. A complete desire has both an altruistic component (the right line), and an egoistic one (the left line). By combining them we "beget" a certain "golden mean," in which two opposite halves come together, forming one middle line: a single desire directed upward, to the spiritual world.

This method ensures the integrity of the entire creature. In other words, not a single force is wasted, not a single word is redundant. Rather, it's all about the correct application of all the forces and processes that take place in man.

Our tiny desire can be likened to a newborn baby; it is already outside its mother's womb, "outside the ark." This "newborn" is that tiny spiritual desire of ours that begins to explore the next degree of correction, called "nursing." The newborn still can't walk, but it is already breathing the air of the earth, demanding sustenance and "kicking its feet." This means that our desire to bestow can be given a tiny dash of egoism, which it can deal with and correct.

We are embarking on a path of correction. Though this desire is only an "infant" now, it will grow into "the leader of the new generation," meaning he will lead your other, yet uncorrected desires to correction, to the Creator.

"And the dove came in to him [to Noah] at eventide; and lo in her mouth an olive-leaf freshly plucked; so Noah knew that the waters were abated from off the earth." This means that you can now get to work. It's time to go ashore and start working with the ego, carefully at first, to ensure it doesn't ruin the young and fragile altruistic blossoms...

What is the freshly plucked olive leaf in the dove's mouth? An olive leaf symbolizes the Light of life, which can only be received in an altruistic desire.

The Noah inside you receives a report: "You can deal with (correct) the little egoistic desires, for you have been sufficiently washed over with water (Light of Mercy). As evidence of this, you are shown this olive leaf (luminescence)."

It's not yet olive oil, which symbolizes the complete Light of Life, nor is it olives, but merely an olive leaf (not light, but luminescence). However, it's enough to begin correcting the small egoistic desires.

"And God spoke unto Noah, saying, 'Go forth... and be fruitful and multiply upon the earth.'" You have overcome this phase of correction called the "ark." You have endured and matured through it; you have essentially been born anew, so now you can be certain that there will not be any more floods. This is the blessing that the Creator gave to "Noah and his sons," the corrected altruistic desires: "Be fruitful and multiply upon the earth."

You have passed through this state, and now altruism (the quality of the Creator) joins with egoism (the quality of the creature). Finally you are "setting foot on the earth" and embarking on the blessed path of the correction of the ego. One way or another, everyone must traverse this path! And until the end of correction of the entire ego (the return to the Garden of Eden), your advancement will be aimed only upward.

There is a saying in Kabbalah: "In the spiritual you always rise and never fall." Indeed, you must know that all the ascents and descents you will feel on your spiritual path lead only up the spiritual ladder. Even if it appears that you've stumbled in the darkness or that the night has dragged on too long ("night" refers to states of spiritual descent when the light is absent), know that it is actually helping you on your spiritual path. The only thing required of you is to grab onto everything that you used to "build the ark," and you will feel the arrival of the morning (the ascent).

Why are there such descents? It's because the Creator's quality of bestowal within us has grown strong enough to handle another portion of the ego, which is immediately supplied for correction. The work must not stop. We must undergo complete purification.

This is why there are times when you feel the descents and hear questions from the ego, which you then correct. It continues to assault you with the same old questions: "Why do you need all this? Leave it alone and focus on important things, like making money!"

The ego's questions don't change; they are very logical and earthly, but you are not the same person anymore. You have already gotten a taste of the spiritual state, and you know that the night will invariably change into morning.

From this point on, your entire path, as described in the book, is one of phases of correction of the ego, with the help of the quality of the Creator.

THE NEW EARTH

"And God spoke unto Noah, saying, 'Go forth from the ark, you, and your wife, and your sons, and your sons' wives with you. Bring forth with you every living thing that is with you of all flesh, both fowl, and cattle, and every creeping thing that creeps upon the earth; that they may swarm in the earth, and be fruitful, and multiply upon the earth.'"

Coming out to "the new earth" is what happens to you after the ark. You view the earth differently, finding joy in everything. You begin to realize that everything around you is given to you as aid in your spiritual advancement. They help you and you help them, and any instance of suffering that transpires is there only for adjustment, to keep you from stumbling by reminding you that everything comes from one source—the Creator.

The suffering is now mitigated by your understanding that it's for your own benefit. It allows you to verify where you are and how far you've deviated from the right path. You get to work, adjust your course, and come right back to a new ascent.

We can sum up the whole notion of suffering with a simple example. A terribly thirsty man stands before a stream of pure spring water, trying to fill up his dirty cup. The water tastes disgusting and bitter to him. He cannot drink it, and he curses the dirty stream (as we often curse the Creator, who sends us suffering). When the man finally realizes that the problem is not with the water, but with his cup, he cleans his cup and the water tastes wonderful.

It is the same with us. People concern themselves only with their corporeal tribulations and curse the suffering that befalls them. They immerse themselves in their problems, blaming everyone around them. But those in whom the point in the heart awakens—who begin to seek entrance into the spiritual world—learn that suffering is helpful because it identifies the spot (desire) that needs checking and cleansing (correction). And the correction is done only by finding the right intention.

The desire remains, only the intention changes. You are no longer waiting for the next blow to come, but instead you actively try to make contact with the Upper One so He wouldn't need to push or adjust your path. You advance upward joyously and without pain to where the infinite, pure Light of love and goodness awaits.

This Light is intended for you; the stream is always flowing with pure spring water for any who thirst for it. Understanding this concept is symbolized by Noah "going forth from the ark onto the new earth."

It is a "new earth" because the earth that was cursed by the Creator (your egoistic desires) began to yield fruit (egoistic desires joined with altruistic ones), enabling life to appear, which steadily brings man to the goal of Creation.

"And God said, 'This is the token of the covenant which I make between Me and you and every living creature that is with you, for perpetual generations: I have set My bow in the cloud, and it shall be for a token of a covenant between Me and the earth.'"

The bow in the cloud (a rainbow) is a restriction that the Creator takes upon Himself not to hold a true judgment over man: to not make any more floods and ruins, but despite your actions (for you are still egoistic by nature) to lead you only to maximum correction.

The Creator pledges to lead you through the good path, the path of love, even though you may perceive this path as fraught with suffering. (Remember the example of the dirty vessel and the pure water. You are the dirty vessel, while He is the pure water. Start cleaning your vessel and you will come to savor the water's true taste.)

A few more words about the rainbow. The rainbow has seven colors. What does that mean? The seven colors denote the seven qualities (*Sephirot*) that comprise our small but complete desire, the combination of the qualities of bestowal and reception—the Creator and the creature.

"And the sons of Noah that went forth from the ark were Shem, and Ham, and Japheth; and Ham is the father of Canaan. These three were the sons of Noah, and of these was the whole earth overspread." Your corrected desires are called "sons." At first there are three of them (referring to the three lines. The right line is from the Creator, the left is from the creature, and the middle line is the result of their union).

The three sons beget all life on the earth. "Life" is everything that opposes egoism. If at times things around you appear lifeless—not opposing the ego, but self-serving, leading to ruin and death and tearing the world apart—stop, think about the goal, and continue your work on correcting yourself and the world. Everything is created with only one goal—to rejoin the Creator.

Believe me, dear reader, it's about to be revealed to you. And one other vitally important thing will be revealed to you: everything is governed by one law—the Law of Love!

"And the whole earth was of one language and of one speech." As you can see, after the "flood," all the desires are aimed only at the Creator. Together they form a single whole between themselves and Nature. All our desires ("bathed" in the Light of mercy) "speak" the same language—the language of love for the Creator.

However, there is still a great deal of work ahead of these first altruistic desires. They must move toward egoistic desires, mix with them, and begin to correct them, starting with the easier ones and moving on to the harder ones, until the entire ego has been corrected. The goal is to "cleanse the vessel" completely. But that will happen later. For now we are only at the beginning of the path.

"And it came to pass, as they journeyed east, that they found a plain in the land of Shinar; and they dwelt there."

As with any reference to movement, "they journeyed east" signifies the attainment of a new spiritual degree. To "settle" or "dwell" means to mix with the new egoistic desires that manifest at that next degree. This is where the infiltration of one desire into another leads to unexpected consequences.

BUILDING THE TOWER OF BABEL

"And they said, 'Come, let us build us a city, and a tower, with its top in heaven, and let us make us a name; lest we be scattered abroad upon the face of the whole earth.'"

And there it is—the first and incredibly significant event that turned the whole world upside down—the beginning of the construction of the Tower of Babel. It is a story that took place some 4,000 years ago, yet remains startlingly topical to this day. So, let us analyze it from all angles.

Even though this event was mentioned at the very beginning of our narrative, let's step back and set the historical backdrop, which proves one thing conclusively: everything that transpires in the material world takes its root from the spiritual one. Any historic event you can think of is a consequence of what has already transpired in the spiritual realm.

There is a saying in Kabbalah that "there is not a blade of grass below that does not have an angel above that strikes it and tells it, 'Grow!'" So is the case with the Tower of Babel. It actually existed, as the annals of history confirm.

At the turn of the 20th century, German archeologist Robert Koldewey discovered the ancient city of Babylon in today's Iraq. It contained the ruins of a tower whose dimensions measured (in meters) 90x90x90. Herodotus, the ancient Greek historian who lived in the 5th century BC, described the tower as a seven-tier pyramid of analogous dimensions. Historical sources speak of the temple complex Esagila, at the heart of which stood the Tower of Babel, dedicated to the god Marduk. It was called Etemenaki, which is Sumerian for "Temple of the Foundation of Heaven and Earth."

Esagila was the religious center of that world, in which paganism reigned. Astrology, zodiac signs and horoscopes, fortune-telling, numerology, spiritism, magic, sorcery, charms, hexes, invocations, exorcism of evil spirits—were all born in Esagila and survive through the modern age. Today, we see a resurgence of these beliefs.

THE BIRTH OF LANGUAGES

There is a hypothesis that Indo-European languages originated from a language spoken by humanity at the age of the construction of the Tower of Babel.

Dr. Russell Gray from Auckland University in New Zealand calculated the approximate "age" of 87 Indo-European languages and concluded that they most likely arose in the period of the Tower of Babel, from which they later migrated west into Europe and east into India.

THE TOWER OF BABEL WITHIN US

The above findings are actually hypotheses about the physical evidence of the existence of the Tower of Babel. We, however, are more interested in the roots of what really happened. We strive to understand the cause, correlate it with our inner world, and make sure that the division that took place then doesn't repeat itself. By attaining the spiritual worlds we can influence the cause of everything that transpires, and thereby change our fate, the fate of the world, and the fate of humanity as a whole.

So the residents of Babylon decide to build a "tower to the heavens." In the interest of clarity and further proof, let us refer to the words of the oral Torah (Midrash), which is based entirely on interpreting the written Torah. This is what the Midrash tells us on the subject: The Babylonians knew the story of the flood. They lived in fear that the same fate might befall them. Thus, they sought a place where they could dwell in complete safety. Ultimately, they found a valley in the land of Babylon that was big enough to hold them all.

Afterwards the people crowned Nimrod as their king. And since they all settled in Babylon, Nimrod essentially became king of the entire population on Earth.

Nimrod proposed to the people, "Let us build a big city where we can all live. And in that city let us erect a very high tower." His subjects were delighted with the idea. He said, "Let us build a tower so high that its top will reach the Heavens, and let us make us a name, lest another flood comes and scatters us throughout the world."

However, though all were united in the belief that the tower must be built, their opinions concerning the purpose of its construction differed. Some people thought, "In the event of another flood, we shall climb to the top of the tower, where the water shall not reach us." Another group thought, "We shall make us a name," aiming to build a place of assembly at the top of the tower and worship their gods there, thus being saved from any calamity. Others still protested, "It is unjust that the Creator alone is lord over the realms above, limiting our domain to the world below."

Do you see the ego talking?! "We will reach the heavens on our own, without the Creator's help. We will rule the world, and not Him. We will build us a tower so high that its top will reach the heavens, and we will make us a name."

Where is this audacity coming from? The answer is that they had reached a new degree. Precisely because they were able to complete the previous degree, they were given additional egoism to work with. At this new degree the ego is king, and its name is "Nimrod," from the word,

Meridah—rebellion. "And so, the people crowned Nimrod to be their king. And since they all settled in Babylon, Nimrod essentially became king of the entire population of Earth."

"Nimrod" is a powerful new egoistic force that rules over the entire ego. And that force is what you must battle now.

FALLING IN ORDER TO RISE

The first thing you experience is descent. "Day" becomes "night," and a feeling overtakes you that the egoistic force of the new degree is winning. Everything you've already attained seems forgotten: it's as if you've never "survived the flood," as though "Noah and his sons" have never existed. Your desire to bestow is powerless before the power of "Nimrod."

(Historically, at this time Babylon undergoes a powerful leap of egoism, which transforms the whole world.)

You may ask, "Is the descent really necessary?" Yes, it is! Moreover, it should be celebrated because it is now that the next rung on the spiritual ladder is born. A new degree is revealed within you.

Actually, it's exactly what happens in life. Imagine that you're the manager of a small company branch. You know everything about your staff. Everyone is friendly and close-knit, celebrating the holidays together, gossiping together about each other, when suddenly you are offered a promotion you cannot resist: you have been transferred to corporate headquarters.

Here come the sleepless nights and nagging thoughts: "Why did I agree to this, sacrificing the peace and happiness I had before?"

It's a new degree. And with a new degree you need to get accustomed to new conditions and new egoistic desires: a higher salary, the wish to be liked by your new superiors and subordinates, and the hope that more promotions lie ahead, provided you succeed. There's no escaping this, since you're dealing with another, higher degree.

That is an example taken from our egoistic world.

In the spiritual world, a new degree is always preceded by a descent. For those who understand that a descent essentially marks the beginning of another ascent, it is a joyous occasion. You already know that after processing a certain portion of the ego, another portion will be added, signaling a new ascent and thus a greater revelation of the Creator. And this inspires you.

The great Kabbalist, Rabbi Shimon Bar Yohai (RASHBI), author of *The Book of Zohar*, enjoyed spiritual heights we cannot even imagine. But prior to each ascent to a new degree, he experienced a descent. And before he ascended to the final, 125th degree, his descent was so deep that the author of the single most celebrated work of Kabbalah felt like an illiterate market hawker, without any spiritual attainment whatsoever. He even forgot the alphabet!

The difference between him and other people that experience descents is that he knew for certain that this state would soon pass, for it preceded his transition on to an even higher degree. You need only to hold on, since before every ascent you are given an additional portion of the ego that must be corrected.

One can never know what lies ahead in the spiritual world. Every new degree is a journey into the unknown. The lower one cannot attain the Upper One until the latter raises him to His level. As was mentioned earlier, you attain the name of a degree, which is one of the Creator's names, only once you've attained the degree itself.

From the aforementioned, it follows that in the spiritual worlds there are only ascents. And even the sensation of a descent constitutes yet another ascent on the path to the goal.

THE BABYLON OF YESTERDAY AND TODAY

Let us return to Babylon. What do we see? At first glance, the ego (Nimrod and his people) appears to have won.

By the way, if we say that by attaining a new degree we discover new names of the Creator, it follows that "Nimrod" is one of His names. Why? Because there is no other force in the world. It is the Creator who puts obstacles on our way toward the goal, and we must overcome them. This is how He rears us and purifies us, because we need to merit the abundance that awaits us at the end of our journey.

The building of the tower was a mammoth undertaking. Because there was no stone in Babylon, the people created a new construction material: they burned clay in fire and used the resulting bricks in place of stone.

The bricks were fashioned as if by themselves: when the people laid one brick, they discovered two in the wall, and when they laid two, four bricks appeared in the wall.

What does this passage mean? It is the voice of the ego (King Nimrod and his people), saying, "We don't need the Upper Force, we'll develop construction technology, we'll believe only in our own hands, in our own intellect, and we will win."

"Because there was no stone in Babylon, the people created a new construction material." Isn't that the same thing that is happening now? But where are we going with this progress? "...they burned clay in the fire and used the resulting bricks in place of stone."

A similar scenario unfolded in early 20th century Russia, when the communists refused to acknowledge the Upper Force, and thought that they could implement their ideas all on their own. On the face of it, those slogans of love, brotherhood, and equality sounded wonderful (the ego is quite cunning). But there was no Upper Force behind those slogans. It was all built upon the earth, meaning founded on the ego.

The Russians didn't realize that man is inherently egoistic, and that sooner or later everything would implode and the Paradise they expected would become Hell.

Until recently, similar developments were happening worldwide, especially in America, until the new process of consciousness began. Now humanity is beginning to understand that no progress can ever lead to happiness if it lacks a connection with the Upper Force.

At first it may appear like it will work, that progress might reduce our workday from twelve hours to five, that we might have more time to spend with our families, to read, educate, and otherwise improve ourselves. Indeed, at first, things appeared to be going wonderfully, and it seemed that we could accomplish anything we put our minds to.

"The bricks were fashioned as if by themselves: when the people laid one brick, they discovered two in the wall, and when they laid two, four bricks appeared in the wall." But what was the end result? Today we work more than ever before; we've become slaves to corporations; our families are breaking up, divorce rates are skyrocketing, which results in miserable adults and children. We seek oblivion in drugs and alcohol and we fall into depression, which has become the most widespread illness of our time. Truly, cavemen were happier than we!

It is the result of progress that is disconnected from the Creator, from the correction of man, and from achieving the quality of bestowal.

So what did progress give us? We are beginning to see that we cannot exist without a connection to the Creator. This is the single most important result of progress.

Until we realize the necessity of correcting the ego, nothing can be done about it. As long as we aren't corrected or involved in the process of correction, we will remain susceptible to the tricks of the ego (Nimrod at the phase of constructing the Tower of Babel, Pharaoh at the phase of Egypt), and the ego will not be denied. It will wage war, push the red button, accept bribes, and throw anyone under the bus, as long as its interests are served, for the ego is corrupt.

I am confident that the world is almost ready to conclude that only the Upper Force can tame the ego. Soon we will all need to turn to the Creator, for we will have no other choice. And yet, it is better to do it in advance and avoid incredible suffering by realizing that we need to connect to the Light, to the Upper Governing Force, and secure its direction.

The tower grew and grew, and soon became so tall that it took a year to climb to its top. Two broad staircases led to the tower, one from the east and one from the west. The staircase to the east was used to lift loads, while the staircase to the west was used to lower people. People needed to go up and down frequently to supply the construction materials.

The builders were so fanatical in their desire to complete the tower that whenever a brick fell and broke, they lamented: "How hard it will be to replace it." "But when a person slipped and fell to his death, no one looked upon him."

At this first phase, this is how the ego quells any buds of selflessness: "But when a person slipped and fell to his death, no one looked upon him."

We've already mentioned that man (Adam) stems from the word *Adameh*—"I will be like" the Creator. Nimrod's people didn't need anything similar to the Creator, only the bricks for construction. Reflect on these words and try to feel them: "But when a person slipped and fell to his death, no one looked upon him."

One day, a man named Abraham, son of Terah, was walking past the site of the tower's construction. He was forty-eight years old at the time, and famous for opposing the erection of the tower. When he approached and was asked, "Join us in building the tower, for you are a powerful man and will be very useful," he refused them, saying, "You have renounced the Creator, who is the Tower, and decided to replace Him with a tower of bricks."

This is how the altruistic force that corresponds to this egoistic degree manifests in us. This force is the only one capable of defeating Nimrod, and its name is Abraham.

This force throws out a warning almost in passing. It is not yet capable of dealing with the enlarged egoism, but its voice can already be heard, and this is very important.

In other words, you are beginning to come alive and exit the state of descent. Armed with new altruistic powers, you are getting to work.

In the meantime, the affair is coming to a head—the tower is about to "collapse." (Indeed, you cannot build anything that's founded on egoism, but only on a connection with the Upper One.)

WHAT TO DO

The book offers this advice: "Listen to the Abraham in you." Find him amidst the egoistic madness and give him the freedom to act. Let the ego squeal and resist any changes aimed at spiritual advancement, but it must be understood that there is no other way. Everything else has been tried and tested, and we can clearly see that it hasn't worked.

Make up your mind, and everything will work out. The Abraham of today will reveal himself to the world.

This is precisely why the wisdom of Kabbalah, hidden from humanity for millennia, is being revealed today.

If humanity listens, we will follow the constructive path of unification with Nature. If it doesn't, we will follow the path of suffering. But either way, we will reach the goal.

What does it mean to unite with Nature? Kabbalists wrote about it almost 4,000 years ago in *The Book of Creation*.

All around us exists a single law, to which we do not conform. The Law of Nature is one of absolute altruism, absolute love. It acts all around us in full force. It is known as the Creator's Law.

What about us? We oppose this law egoistically. Instead of correcting our constantly growing egos and equalizing with Nature, we put up artificial barriers to protect ourselves from it. That is what all our sciences and technologies are used for.

This phenomenon of man refusing to correct himself and seeking to dominate Nature instead is what's referred to as "building the Tower of Babel."

Since the days of Babylon, our egos have been gradually developing until they have reached their peak. Humanity has become disillusioned with its ability to satiate its own ego via technological or any other kind of progress. Today we are beginning to realize that this whole journey of ours was trekked in vain.

Due to the crisis and the dead end we find ourselves in, you could say that the ruin of the Tower of Babel is happening before our very eyes. Now all we need is to make the right choice. After all, haven't we made enough bad choices and suffered for it?

The great Kabbalist, Yehuda Ashlag, known as Baal HaSulam (Owner of the Ladder) for his *Sulam* (Ladder) commentary on *The Book of Zohar*, wrote in the 1940s that if humanity didn't come to its senses there would be a third and then a fourth world war, with only a handful of survivors. These people will then unify with the universal law, and the world will know true peace and love.

As always, we need to translate these words into the language of the Kabbalah. When the ego isn't tearing you apart from the inside, you are ready and willing to give yourself over to others, and love is the product of bestowal that is felt by both sides.

"In the end, the Creator descended upon the earth with seventy angels and held court over that generation." This passage speaks of the altruistic force (the Creator) "descending upon the earth" as a result of the breaking. In other words, this force entered the egoistic desire (the earth).

Don't let phrases like "held court over that generation" scare you. It simply means that we suddenly saw ourselves the way we really are. This was made possible by the light of the altruistic sparks that entered us. Like flashlight beams, they illuminated the darkness and granted us sight, and we realized that all our actions are dictated exclusively by self-love.

"I am an egoist!" This single egoistic sensation comprises seventy individual egoistic desires (70 Sephirot).

Each of these desires was infiltrated by an altruistic spark during the breaking, turning our whole lives upside down, demolishing the usual order of things, and forcing us to reflect on who we are.

Imagine how shocked people were when they suddenly discovered that they couldn't communicate with each other in one language and were instead inexplicably speaking seventy different languages.

In other words, in the illumination of the altruistic Light, it was discovered that every desire lives only for itself. This is how all people live. No one understands another, and all the slogans about love and brotherhood are empty words. The true altruism highlighted the abyss that truly exists between egoistic desires—people, nations, and the world—and showed that egoism does not allow us to love, be together, or speak the same language. Egoism is when everyone cares only for themselves, speaking their own language that others cannot understand.

The mixing of the languages happened instantly. People addressed one another, but couldn't understand a single word. One said, "Give me water!" Instead, he was handed clay. Another demanded, "Give me a rope!" Instead, he was handed a saw. In one case, a man who received a saw instead of a rope struck the man who misunderstood him, killing him. A terrible discord and turmoil fell upon the land. The people all picked up arms and began to kill their friends— and so perished half of humanity.

In the altruistic Light, it becomes evident that the ego has no friends. It is designed to drive us to the extreme, pinning us to the wall. Only then do we realize that we are trapped, slaves to the ego without any free will of our own, realizing that everything we had done throughout our lives was at the command of self-love.

Man suddenly discovers that instead of creating, he was "killing" all along. Entrenched in terrorism and drugs, feeling helpless and unfulfilled, he is ultimately brought to a desperate state. He doesn't see a way out and doesn't want to move in any direction. He has become so distant from Nature that he doesn't see from where salvation might come or what he can do. This realization constitutes the "ruin of the Tower of Babel" within us.

What happens next? Next, a wisdom known as Kabbalah comes to the rescue. This wisdom was born back in the age of Ancient Babylon, was kept secret for thousands of years, and is now being revealed throughout the world, for humanity will never know how to continue to develop without it. Things will continue to deteriorate until humanity is ready to utilize the method of the world's correction as a solution to all the problems.

Meanwhile, we've come to the end of the chapter about Noah. Next, we will look into the chapter, *Lech Lecha* (Go Forth).

CHAPTER 3

GO FORTH

Dear reader, you are about to ascend to the next egoistic degree. New characters enter the stage, which are your new desires. Their goal is simple—to help you achieve the most perfect state imaginable.

However, in order to continue our journey within ourselves, you must step back to the time when you were certain you could do it all on your own, build it all with your own hands, and achieve happiness without any help from outside. But that was before the ruin of the Tower of Babel inside you.

THE KINGDOM OF EGOISM

At that time, a king named Nimrod (your ego) reigned within you. You followed him faithfully, trusted him, and worshipped only him.

Here is a description of this period from the Midrash: "The strength and cunningness of King Nimrod became proverbial. Everyone knew that his arm, aimed at a deer's heart, never missed its target. Woe was he who dared to question that Nimrod was a self-made god, for an executioner always stood by the side of his throne."

The Nimrod inside you refers to the natural, fairly developed egoism that wishes for, and can achieve, anything: "Everyone knew that his arm, aimed at a deer's heart, never missed its target."

If you remember, your entire life and all your intentions were focused exclusively on yourself. "What does it do for me" was the principle you lived by. All of your relations with others essentially came down to this.

"Nimrod" was always your essence. He didn't take anyone into account but himself: "Woe was he who dared to question that Nimrod was a self-made god."

In other words, "I'm OK with everything else existing, as long as it exists under me! I'm willing to accept everything, I'm willing to pay, but I must be above it all! Because it cannot be that someone has created me!" This was the reasoning of your ego: "Nimrod was a self-made god."

"I come first" was how you felt. You didn't acknowledge anyone else, as your inner "Nimrod" ran the show from atop his throne.

The "throne" signifies power. It is the "Tower of Babel" inside you resisting the Creator and rebelling against Him.

At the time, you didn't know that it wouldn't last, that your Nimrod would fail, "...for an executioner always stood by the side of his throne."

The executioner who always stands by the side of the throne is your sentiment that anything slightly offensive to the ego, seeking to somehow obstruct, curb, or oppress it, is subject to immediate extermination.

Your Nimrod doesn't tolerate any opposition to his rule. Remember the times in your life when you felt particularly pained or upset? That happened when your very essence was attacked. You felt humiliated whenever someone infringed upon your "I," debasing the "holy of holies," "the god Nimrod" inside you.

THE PROPHECY

The Midrash goes on to say, "One day Nimrod's astrologists approached the throne reverently and prostrated before the king. 'Oh, great lord,' they proclaimed, 'We come with news of great peril which threatens your rule. The stars foresee that a boy will soon be born in your kingdom who shall deny your divinity and shall defeat you.'"

Nimrod's astrologists are your own fear, dear reader, which exists within the ego itself. The fear is that something may shake your foundation, your Nimrod. This fear is always driving your ego to worry about its fulfillment and prosperity, seeking more stuff, bigger stuff, newer stuff. And yet, this perpetual drive to fulfill yourself ultimately brings you to a point where a "boy is born" inside you that will one day defeat Nimrod.

Who is this boy who will be born inside you? It is the budding of the next degree. It arises from that same Nimrod, from your "I," which suddenly begins to understand that being a Nimrod is nothing but misery. All of a sudden you realize that your life is far from cloudless, since you're always concerned: concerned with building yourself on the ruin of others, with protecting your "I" from attacks, and with staying on top, on your throne.

At the same time, you cannot destroy everyone who threatens you. Otherwise, whom will you dominate?

It follows that your ego is completely and absolutely dependent on those in your environment, and we see many examples of this. For instance, take movie stars or other celebrities flashing their perfect smiles—a testament to their absolute happiness. But is that really so? For all of their massive incomes, they are still very much dependent on the press, on their producers and directors, and on the public—in short, on everyone around them. They often break under the pressure and lapse into drug or alcohol dependencies in a desperate attempt to find a way out of the cage that their own egos landed them in.

"Nimrod" is in power, demanding to always be worshipped. "Do whatever it takes to make others respect you," your ego keeps murmuring.

You cannot destroy your environment. You cannot erase their "I." And even if you could, you wouldn't, because then you'd have no one to rule over. After all, you neither can nor want to demonstrate your superiority to a herd of cows. No, you need to be surrounded by intellectuals; it is them you want, not a herd of cows bowing down before you. Only then does the ego thrive. It follows that your Nimrod is incredibly dependent on other people. He must support them, pay them, nurture them, and at the same time, oppress them.

Indeed, the ego rises precisely when it oppresses others. Hence, the next degree of the ego's (Nimrod's) development in you is when it begins to recognize its own dependence, vulnerability, and fragility.

This process is called "the recognition of evil in Nimrod." It is when you finally get the feeling that your freedom is somehow restricted.

You are dependent on everybody else. That is the problem of kings, presidents, and whoever else might be in power. But in reality, it is the problem of every person. You must always build a pyramid around you, but in a way that always keeps you on top. You need to have the respect of your children, wife, relatives, co-workers, passengers on the bus or other means of public transportation, even your neighbor's dog barking at you. But how long can you keep up with this game?!

So your next degree is Abraham. He is freedom, he is ascent, he is the revolutionary idea that comes to you after all the suffering, and the discoveries that bestowal, not reception, must be the sole purpose of your existence. He wants to deny and discard all the lies and excesses! This is the new degree arising in you, in your Nimrod.

It follows that Abraham cannot exist without Nimrod. Nimrod is the degree preceding Abraham. Nimrod is the exorbitant ego that realizes that its ultimate destiny is self-destruction, unless it can find a new system of fulfillment, that is, unless it can rise above itself.

Now let us continue our story. "One day Nimrod's astrologists approached the throne reverently and prostrated before the king." Who are Nimrod's astrologists? They are forces in your ego that vow that you cannot continue living as you were. They are intermediary states that predict, foresee, and anticipate the next degree that Abraham should become.

So, the astrologists inside you are the intermediary state between Nimrod and Abraham.

"The stars foresee that a boy will soon be born in your kingdom who shall deny your divinity and shall defeat you." What do the "stars" symbolize? These are the forces of your inner development. It is useless to resist them. It will be as they say, even if you are King Nimrod himself. You cannot circumvent them. Sooner or later, one way or the other, egoism will give way to altruism, and you will be happy. You will reveal the spiritual world and accept its laws. That is the only goal they're guiding you toward, no matter what you do—they will get you there!

Nimrod turned to his ministers. "What protective measures do you suggest?" The answer came quickly, "Issue a decree to have all newborn boys put to death!" "A wonderful suggestion! Call a meeting of architects. I shall issue an order to construct special houses that will keep all the pregnant women. We need to make sure that only girls are left alive."

Fear not, dear reader, but keep on trying to get at the inner meaning of what is going on here. To start with, let us clarify that "son" or "boy" in Hebrew is *Ben*. The word *Ben* comes from the word *Mevin*—"understanding" or "attainment." Attainment of what? The new degree. And that is what Nimrod fears so much. That is what poses a threat to his power. To protect itself, the ego must eradicate attainment, allegorically expressed in killing newborn boys.

"We need to make sure that only girls are left alive." Girls, daughters, the feminine part in you, is the personification of the desire to receive. This is why your Nimrod is so fond of the notion of women giving birth to girls. In other words, the more new desires appear in you, the more they will add to Nimrod's glory and add to his growing authority and dominion—and that's something Nimrod has no problem with.

What he does have a problem with is another method of fulfilling the desires, a new method for receiving pleasure that is born in the form of Abraham.

Let us try to step outside ourselves for a moment and examine ourselves. Our desires grow, meaning that girls are born to us. But one day we notice that the desires change *qualitatively*. We are no longer satisfied with the previous fulfillments. It is no longer enough to plop down on the couch with a beer and watch TV. Wealth no longer brings the same satisfaction. The pleasure of being a big boss grows stale, and the achievements and acquisitions from before no longer fulfill our desires!

This means that our desires not only grew, but changed in quality, and now we want a different kind of fulfillment. We want it, but fear it at the same time because we understand that it will turn our lives entirely upside down. That's Nimrod rebelling within us! That is how he concludes that all similar thoughts must be destroyed.

But can he destroy them? From our Nimrod, from our very own unfulfilled ego rises a new generation, and this process cannot be stopped!

The girls (desires) and boys (ways of fulfilling them) that are born within us pertain to a new degree. In Kabbalah, it is called the degree of *Bina* within us. *Bina* is the degree of bestowal, love, and mercy. Through this process we learn that at this degree we can feel infinitely more pleasure. In fact, we can feel infinity itself.

Listen to your inner Nimrod. It is telling you, "Fine, I'm willing to bestow. I will do it, but only because it will give me pleasure." "I will feel good," Nimrod thinks to himself, "I will use this part of *Bina* that's in me, this degree of bestowal and infinite pleasures, but I will use it for my own benefit. I will bestow, sure, but only because it serves *my* interests!"

This is called "using the spark of love," the Creator's spark, which exists in all of us, but for our own benefit. This is what "killing the sons" means, receiving the entire Light—all of the tremendous energy of an ascent—for the sake of your own satisfaction.

But as it turns out, it's a doomed endeavor, and the Nimrod inside you is about to realize his folly. He still hasn't realized it, and so he welcomes the birth of girls (desires of the new degree), but fights tooth and nail to prevent the birth of Abraham—a new manner of their fulfillment. For now, he still thinks that his plan will work.

Terah, one of Nimrod's most esteemed nobles, asked jokingly, "You don't plan to put my own wife into one of these buildings, do you? She is pregnant as we speak."

"We weren't talking about your household, Terah," the king assured him, "for you are the most trusted of all my ministers."

Terah is "one of the most esteemed nobles," Nimrod's right hand, Nimrod's ideologist, the ego's ideologist. So, the ego inside you grows, and the Terah inside you must find a new way to manage this growing ego in a way that you can continue to feel pleasure.

Terah represents the method of fulfilling a desire. Therefore, we need to spend a little time on the man called Terah, the ego's ideologist, to understand how he could beget the Abraham inside you.

THE BIRTH OF ABRAHAM INSIDE YOU

The birth of Abraham is the inner revolution that takes place in Terah. It is the actual method of fulfilling Nimrod. This event symbolizes the fact that it is impossible to fulfill yourself as before at the new degree of the growing ego. The method of fulfillment itself needs drastic change. This revolution is known as Abraham.

So Terah begets Abraham to completely revamp the method of fulfilling his ego, the Nimrod in him.

One morning, Nimrod's astrologists request an audience with him once again. "The threat has not been neutralized, oh, King! We have observed above Terah's house a star, dashing about the firmament in all directions. It devoured four stars to the east, to the north, to the west and to the south. This clearly points to Terah's new son, who will conquer your kingdom!"

The "star, dashing about the firmament" inside you is the sign that Abraham stands for bestowal. It is the change from an egoistic intention to one of complete bestowal. From this day forward, the method of Abraham will rule over all four phases of the ego's development, meaning over all of your desires.

"...a star, dashing about the firmament in all directions. It devoured four stars to the east, to the north, to the west, and to the south." From the moment Abraham is born, deep within the bowels of your ego you begin to realize that all the things that used to fulfill you before are senseless. Your possessions no longer satisfy you; life has lost its flavor, and former pleasures are empty. Frantically, you search for a way out of this dead end.

This is how a completely new approach (star) is born within you. It is a new way of fulfilling your desire, a new method that turns a new page in your life and actualizes all the new desires created in you (north, south, west, and east). It is a happy time for you, for a new intention to bestow is born within you.

The Midrash goes on to say that a boy is born to Terah, and given the name Abraham. But you already know that Abraham is born inside you. That is the true and only meaning of this story.

DISCOVERIES MADE IN A CAVE

What are the growth conditions you must provide for your Abraham? You must put him in a cave. So says the Midrash: "Terah orders him to be hidden in a cave." What does it mean to hide your newborn Abraham (intention to bestow) in a cave? It means to create in the earth, in your own ego, a special place in which Abraham (*Bina*, the part of the Creator in you, the intention to bestow) can develop.

In other words, in this egoistic, material world, filled with corrupt calculations and hatred, where people exploit one another for personal profit, you must dig a cave for yourself, meaning choose a special environment. You must find like-minded friends who also aspire to the spiritual, books that describe the exalted, spiritual worlds, and a guide who will lead you toward the spiritual goal. If you do this, it will mean that you have dug a cave in the earth.

Remember that Noah—the first desire for the spiritual that arose at the smallest egoistic level—took the same approach. The book of Genesis states that Noah entered the ark as though it were a cave, a ship that sails along the waters, and that ensured his salvation. He was able to avoid being saturated with the values of this egoistic world, and later came out onto an earth that had been purified by the flood waters.

So it is now, at the new degree of the ego's development. History repeats itself, only the growth of Abraham inside you takes place not on an ark, but in a cave. He is raised in a special environment, which is why it is written: "The young Abraham grew up in a cave, far away from the boisterous world of people. Possessing an extraordinary mind, he came to know the Creator when he was only three years of age."

Why "three years of age"? It denotes the first phase of development of the Abraham inside you. It is the period of his birth. As we've already mentioned, at the higher level of the ego's development, a new method of sensing the spiritual is born within you. The next phase is called "nursing."

While "in the cave," your inner Abraham undergoes this period of nursing in his environment, reading the works of great sages, listening to the teacher's guidance and striving to follow it. The third phase (three years) signifies understanding, the phase of *Bina*, the sensation of the spiritual, the realization that everything in this world is governed by the Upper Force, which leads the world toward its best possible state.

The Abraham inside you comes to understand this. Hold on to your Abraham; he knows where he must bring you.

It is written: "Moreover, he did it on his own, having reached this conclusion by way of observation and reasoning." Observation is the continual development of the quality of *Bina* within you, the Creator's quality. As you already know, *Bina* derives from the word *Mevin* or *Havana*, which translates as "understanding."

Thus the method continues to develop. The phase of Abraham, the degree of *Bina*, operates inside you, and you are drawing closer and closer to the Creator.

"Perhaps I should worship the earth," he reasoned, "for man is nourished by its fruits? Yet the earth is not all-powerful, but is dependent on the heavens, which bestow the rain. Should I therefore worship the firmament? It is clear that the firmament is governed by the sun, whose warmth and light sustains the world's livelihood."

Abraham prostrated himself before the sun. But when the night fell and the sun gave way to the moon, Abraham reasoned that the moon may be no less divine. But he relinquished that thought as well, judging that since the moon only shines at night, it cannot be more powerful than the sun, which only shines during the day.

You understand that growth can only happen thanks to changes in your inner states: from "day," when everything is clear and the spiritual goal is of utmost importance in your life, to "night," when doubts come and you must find within you the strength to give the ego a good punch in the teeth. Darkness is essential to your growth. Out of Nimrod rises Terah, out of Terah rises Abraham, and so on.

And so you cleanse, passing through all these states. Night replaces day, which is again followed by night, though already at a different phase of your understanding (or observation). And so, together with your Abraham, you perceive that only one force governs the world, and this force is one of love and bestowal—the Creator. And Abraham is its spark.

The most important insight that you've gained by your observations is that egoism in and of itself is not evil. Using egoism for your own benefit, however, is evil. But if you were to use it for the sake of others, you would cease to perceive it as evil. It is as if you shed your old skin, your ego becomes constructive, and you derive pleasure from its constructive nature.

So what's changed? Your intention has changed. The ego has stopped being destructive, and has become constructive. You realize that "I delight in bestowing. The pleasures that awaken in me now are eternal and never-ending, for they don't neutralize the desire to bestow."

This is what a simple intention called "Abraham" does—it offers you a way to be happy. You now understand that the essences of desire and intention are completely different. The intention pertains to thought, whereas the desire pertains to its corporeal manifestation.

The moment you truly begin to recognize and categorize these two forces within you, you will feel very clearly that your spiritual vessel is forming. You will begin to identify yourself with intentions, rather than desires.

Your attitude toward the world, toward other people and everything that surrounds you will change drastically. This change will be the result of your ability to categorize everything that happens to you into two distinct domains:

"my desire" and "my intention." You will say to yourself, "I work only with the intention and do not take my desire into account. I don't care one bit what my desires are. I rise above this plane where people are judged by their desires. It's not for me anymore. I deal exclusively with intentions."

This gradual realization that only the intention, and not the desires, over which you have no control, is the foundation upon which you are built. It allows you to see the world and the entire universe with new eyes. Your worldview undergoes a fundamental change. From a receiver, you turn into a giver enabling you to see the true world—the Upper World—to see the Creator.

Abraham drew a conclusion that an all-powerful and wise Creator must be present behind all of this: "It follows that a supernal Intellect must exist, guiding them."

You see how two intentions can exist over one desire. These two intentions are currently at war within you. It's also worth noting that your old intention "for yourself," the root of egoism, is not being destroyed. On the contrary, everything is founded on it. Your gigantic ego is preserved, but is fulfilled in a different way, with the method of Abraham. Thus, in observing these two intentions you arrive at the attainment of the Creator's singularity. This singular Upper Force is the foundation of absolutely everything: night and day, intentions to receive or to bestow—everything is subject to this force.

"I've not seen the Creator," Abraham said, "but I know that only a mighty and merciful God could create this wonderful world around me, and that only His supernal intellect could sustain the existence of this world. It is He whom I will worship!"

You couldn't see this wonderful world while in your egoistic state because you were always worrying about yourself and how to fulfill your ego. How could any world in which you're perpetually pursuing any and all fulfillment—be it money, fame or power—be wonderful? The ego continues to grow, and you must continue to assuage it with more money, more fame, and more power!

But the wonderful world refers to the world that *Abraham* sees. You can see this wonderful world as well, if you merge with your intention to bestow. If you use your egoism correctly you will rise above it, and you'll begin to see the future and your life going forward. All your aspirations are to bestow. That is the meaning of "seeing a wonderful world," to receive for the sake of bestowal.

Abraham is the degree of *Bina* inside you, which is absolute bestowal. That degree is saying, "I don't need anything; I want only to bestow."

But is this state really perfect? You ask yourself, "Where is this ego that I rose above? What happened to it? I haven't fulfilled it as a result of this action, but simply pushed it away from me and rose above it. But I was born an egoist and must learn how to use my egoism."

With this, you ask how to connect your Abraham with your egoistic nature, ensuring that Abraham will then demand to be rewarded with the next degree. He insists, "Give me the opportunity to actualize your absolute desire to bestow, give me a son, so that at this degree I could learn to fulfill my ego through bestowal!"

"I've not seen the Creator," Abraham said, "but I know that only a mighty and merciful God could create this wonderful world around me."

What is the meaning of "I've not seen the Creator"? It means that by connecting with Abraham you connect with the quality of *Hassadim* (mercy) inside you. It's as if you gain the ability to rise above this world and above your ego, without fulfilling it. You simply leave the ego by the wayside. This is why Abraham knew, but didn't "see" the Creator.

So when will you be able to "see" the Creator? Only when the Light of Life (*Ohr Hochma*) enters you. When will that happen? When the Abraham inside you attains new degrees, when "his sons" appear, who won't flee from the ego, but will find a way to fulfill it. In other words, they will do what is essentially the purpose of man: receiving all the pleasures the Creator has prepared for him.

ON IDOLS AND THE CREATOR

Terah, Abraham's father, sold statues of idols, and Abraham did all he could to convince people not to buy them: "One day his father had to leave on a trip, and he left his shop to be looked after by Abraham, who was now grown."

He gave his son the following instructions: "The larger the size of the idol, the higher should be your asking price. If an important person comes in, offer them a larger idol, and to an unimportant customer offer a smaller idol." With these words, Terah departed.

Some time later, an impressive, broad-shouldered man walked into the shop. "Give me a large idol, as befits my standing!" he addressed the boy haughtily. Abraham handed him the largest idol he could find on the shelf, and the man took out a large sum of money from his purse.

"How old are you," Abraham asked him.

"Fifty," the man replied.

"And you're not embarrassed to worship an idol that's only one day old?" Abraham asked. "My father only made it yesterday!"

The man felt ashamed, took his money back and left the shop.

An old woman came in. She said to the young shopkeeper that thieves had come into her house at night and stolen all her idols.

"Is that so," Abraham said. "If your idols are unable to protect themselves from burglars, why do you hope that they will protect you?"

"You are right," the woman admitted. "But whom else shall I serve?"

"The Creator of the heavens and the earth, He who has made me, and you, and all people," Abraham answered.

The woman left the shop without buying anything.

Another woman came in, carrying with her a bowl filled with flour as an offering to idols. Abraham took an axe and shattered all the idols except for the biggest one. When Terah returned and saw the destruction in his shop, he shouted, "What happened here?"

"Why should I conceal the truth from you?" Abraham answered. "While you were gone, a woman came in and made an offering of flour to the idols. Every one of the idols exclaimed that he wanted to eat it first. The biggest idol grew angry, grabbed the axe, and shattered all the others."

"What is this nonsense?" Terah asked angrily, "You know as well as I do that idols don't eat and don't move, to say nothing of fighting."

"Is that right?" Abraham countered. "But if what you say is true, why do you serve them?"

Here your Abraham springs into action. He begins to explain to your other desires, great and small, men and women, about the ego that rules over you. That is, the first time Abraham is revealed in you, it is as a teacher. He says to you the following: "The ego cannot protect you; it cannot raise you or fulfill you. It cannot!"

What's interesting here is that Abraham appeals to you, an egoist, saying that your egoistic desires will never be fulfilled. Or rather, he appeals to the ego to seek out new ways to fulfill itself. The search for self-fulfillment is egoistic, to be sure, but it is precisely this search that will bring you to the Creator. Essentially, the ego willingly embarks on the path of self-destruction.

The great Kabbalist, Baal HaSulam, says the same thing when he explains how emptiness (lack of fulfillment) emerges within man, who then begins to ask, "What do I live for?" "What is the meaning of my life?" Though the questions are egoistic, they end up bringing man to a new way of using his desires, which is no longer egoistic. This is how the ego leads itself toward the goal of its correct utilization.

Why and how does this happen inside you? It's because you are special in that the point in the heart has already awakened within you. You have the quality of *Bina*, which lives inside every one of us. Otherwise you wouldn't be able to grasp this material; you wouldn't have gotten past the first few pages of this book! It is this point of *Bina* that's called the "human" (Adam) within you.

So, the quality of *Bina* gradually begins to point at your ego and tell you that you're using it incorrectly. This is done by the Abraham in you. "You aren't working with your nature correctly, so it cannot protect you or give you anything. It is inanimate, like all of these idols, made simply out of clay."

Let us return to the Midrash: "Abraham took an axe and shattered all the idols except for the biggest one. When Terah returned and saw the destruction in his shop, he shouted, 'What happened here?'"

"Why should I conceal the truth from you?" Abraham answered. "While you were gone, a woman came in and made an offering of flour to the idols. Every one of the idols exclaimed that he wanted to eat it first. The biggest idol grew angry, grabbed the axe and shattered all the others into many pieces."

"What is this nonsense?" Terah asked angrily, "You know as well as I do that the idols don't eat and don't move, to say nothing of fighting."

"Is that right?" Abraham countered. "But if what you say is true, why do you serve them?"

The Terah inside you understands which idols he worships. Let's face it, you understand perfectly that you deify the ego, which you can never fulfill. You understand that these are inanimate desires, which means the Light simply cannot enter them, since the Light's very nature is opposite to them. The Terah in you understands all this, just as you understand that these desires dominate you and you cannot escape them.

You also understand that Abraham is the degree that follows Terah. And that is the most important thing to understand. You understand that you are born an egoist, and you already feel that the only way to defeat your nature is to reveal the Abraham within, the Creator's quality of love, the desire to bestow.

There are two forces within you, battling one another. One says that this is your world, everyone lives this way and there's no escaping it. It is how you were born, and so you must continue to sell and buy "idols," meaning use your ego to receive pleasures, however shallow and transitory they may be. Conversely, the other force is persuading you that all this is a lie, that the whole world, which deifies the ego—the pleasures and all these "idols" that have no divinity to them because they are not connected in any way to the Creator—is false and fictitious.

You don't yet see that inside and behind every single thing in this world stands the Creator, deliberately confusing you. But you are ready to accept the degree of Abraham as a more progressive degree; you understand that it will help you make sense of everything.

It is written in the Midrash that the king ordered his soldiers to find Abraham. Abraham and Terah show up at the castle. "Nimrod sat on his throne." Anyone who approached the throne had to bow down before the king, but when Abraham was led into the throne room, he remained standing.

Nimrod is sitting on the throne because it's your nature, your "I," your essence, which comes down to everything working for your benefit, a foundation that appears unshakable. But your Abraham doesn't want to bow before this ideology of exploiting others for self-gratification.

He admits that his nature is such that he desires pleasure. However, he wishes to use this desire for the sake of others, rather than for himself. He wishes to learn to bestow. And you are with him. This marks your step-by-step breakaway from the egoistic desire, which will later become an order directly from the Creator: "Get thee out of thy country," which means to reject your egoistic desire. We will talk about that later, but for now you are beginning to break away from your ego. You no longer wish to receive any egoistic pleasures.

Once you've achieved this goal by rising above your nature, and have connected with your Abraham, a new and far more complicated phase will begin, but no less necessary. In it, you'll need to reconnect with your ego, but with a different intention. You will delight in bestowing to others.

For now there is an argument between your Abraham and your Nimrod. According to the Midrash, Nimrod said, "My rule extends over the sun, the moon and the stars!"

Abraham replied, "Every day the sun rises in the east and sets in the west. Order the sun tomorrow to rise in the west and set in the east... or [if you are all-powerful] grant me another request. Tell me what I'm thinking right now and what I'm planning on doing." Finally, Abraham concluded in the presence of all the nobles: "You are no god!"

"Guards!" Nimrod cried out, "put this rebel in prison at once!"

What's happening here is that your Abraham wants to show your Nimrod that your ego controls neither itself nor Nature. For all of its confidence in being a god, it knows not the forces that govern it.

We think we are in control because we exist in a state of concealment. Think back to who you were only a little while ago. Didn't you think that you were in complete control, autonomous and free to make your choices? Now Abraham is exposing this delusion, making it clear that you have no control over your actions or fate. Indeed, this is a revelation for your Nimrod.

It follows that without Abraham it is impossible to see your true limitations. And this discovery is far from pleasant.

PRISON

Abraham is thrown into a dungeon for ten years.

Dear reader, I trust you already realized that everything that happens to you in life happens exclusively for your own benefit. Your entire life on this earth is nothing other than your individual journey to the Creator as He leads you to Himself.

The dungeon that your Abraham is thrown into is the optimal state for your development at this time. Your Abraham must realize that he is hopelessly attached to his ego. He must experience it first-hand, not conceptually, but really feel it! And the only way to feel it and clearly see that the ego is an evil force of darkness robbing you of your freedom, is to put yourself "deep into the earth," in the dungeon—the darkest and innermost part of your ego, where you can't help but feel terrible and shackled by it. This can only be done in the prison of the ego, in the bowels of the earth.

I'd like to reiterate that the word "earth" (*Eretz*) derives from the word *Ratzon* (desire). In other words, you are being immersed in the bowels of the earth, deep within your desire. This is an important experience for your Abraham, who must feel and live through it all to break away from the ego.

Here, Abraham is going through a phase that every person who cannot let go of his ego goes through. You try everything in your power to reconcile the ego with what you're studying; you wish to remain an egoist, yet connect to the Creator at the same time. Thus, Abraham finds himself imprisoned.

The period when you feel as though you're languishing in prison is a preparatory one, and it may feel extraordinarily long.

In Kabbalah this state is called "the double concealment of the Creator." This is followed by a period of "single concealment." These are phases of your "imprisonment."

You already know about the existence of the Upper Governance when you are already with Abraham, but you realize that your nature cannot be defeated.

This is the state called "imprisonment," which lasts until you begin to realize that you can regain your freedom, but not by your own efforts. Rather, you can be free only if the Creator rescues you.

It takes time to realize this.

As the Midrash states, your Abraham remains in prison for ten years. Needless to say, we're not talking about corporeal years, for your liberation can happen in an instant. Ten years later, Nimrod finally realizes that Abraham cannot be broken, and orders to have him executed.

THE DEATH THAT DIDN'T HAPPEN

"Nimrod ordered his people to prepare in his capital, Ur of the Chaldeans, a furnace for execution by fire."

"Death" is the departure of the Light. "Death by fire" is when you are given so much Light, so much pleasure, that you can't help but start receiving it for yourself. And when that happens, shame burns you alive. There is nothing more terrible than that.

And that is what awaits your Abraham. He is already on the path to the Creator. He has experienced the bliss of being close to the Light, existing in congruence with the Law of Love and bestowal, and now he is being placed against his will in conditions that may "burn him alive."

Imagine that you've been given everything you could possibly dream of: money, high social status, power and fame, health, and even the sensation that you're advancing toward a spiritual revelation. As they say, it's "an offer you can't refuse." You are bound by egoistic bonds and given time to think about the offer—three days.

"Abraham remained in chains for three days while Nimrod's slaves lay down wood both outside and inside, preparing the furnace for execution."

The "three days" symbolize the three lines. It is when you are overcome with doubts as to what you should choose. Doubts are the chains binding your Abraham. As for what your choice should be, we already said that it's your middle line, also known as "faith above reason."

In this part of the Midrash, we meet Amathlaah, Abraham's mother, for the first time. She comes with a request: "Won't you bow down before Nimrod just one time?" she whispers to Abraham, "and he will pardon you, my darling son."

What is this degree inside you, called "Abraham's mother"? A mother is the degree of egoism that nourishes you. A father signifies intention; a mother is your ego. You haven't left the home of your "father and mother" (your innate desires), which is why your mother can approach you.

As was already mentioned, you are visited by doubts, both natural and dear like a mother, which used to be able to persuade you. This is the final test before your leap onto the next spiritual degree. "Won't you bow down before Nimrod just one time?" "Just take what he wishes to give you one time." To take means to receive pleasure for your own sake, without considering anyone else.

Abraham refuses, and thus tears himself from the previous degree once and for all. Your Abraham proves that he has no connection to his father (former ideology) or his mother (ego's previous degree).

This breakaway epitomizes the beginning of your "I" swiftly moving toward the moment in life when it hears the order: "Go forth from your country, from your relatives and from the home of your father, into the land that I shall show you."

"And then Nimrod's slaves set the pyramid of wood afire from both ends." Nimrod's slaves are those desires that serve your egoism. Who can save you from this predicament? You are weak, while the desires serving Nimrod are powerful. You cannot resist them! You are about to break and "burn down" (from shame, as we've mentioned). And so you pray, really pray, from the very bottom of your heart. And that's when the Creator answers.

"The Creator answered, 'There is none like Me in the heavens, and there is none like Abraham on the earth. I will come down Myself to save him from the fire!' And the Creator Himself willed the flames to not cause Abraham harm.'"

Only the Upper Force can drag you from one degree to the next. When you have no hope left, when your mind is no longer useful, you will decide to go with faith above reason (reason being the ego's faithful servant), when you resolve to rise above it.

This is when a "miracle" happens ("miracle" from the standpoint of egoism, though in full conformity with the spiritual), and the Creator Himself pulls you from one degree onto the other. Another way of saying it would be that you begin to fully identify with *Bina*, the Creator's part in you. You rise "above the earth"—above *Malchut*, above the ego. And the "fire" cannot hurt you anymore.

"The wood transformed into wondrous branches, thick with fruit." You will burn from shame if you use the Light of fulfillment for your own pleasure. However, if you use it for the sake of bestowal, the "wood" that's supposed to burn you up will transform into fruits you can eat, to fill yourself with and thereby advance.

"And Abraham came out unharmed with all eyes on him and the crowd awe-struck." "Why are you still alive?" Nimrod asked, trembling with fear.

"God, Who has created the heavens and the earth, and Whom you have been mocking, saved me from death."

In other words, your Abraham has shown everyone that you can rise above the egoistic desire. Moreover, it is the only way to be liberated from the sordid nature that governs you. You can come out from under it, and then no one will have power over you.

The crowd (all your egoistic desires) now sees that it is possible, for they, too, exist on the level of Nimrod. They understand that they were under the rule of the ego, but didn't see any way of escaping. And now Abraham shows them that there is a way.

"Stunned and terrified, the king prostrated himself before Abraham. All the ministers did the same. 'Do not bow before me,' said Abraham, 'but bow down instead before the living God, Creator of the Universe.'"

In other words, the quality you acquire does not allow you to puff up with pride, for now you understand where your salvation comes from, and you direct everyone to this source of life, to the Creator, the quality of bestowal, the Light that is revealed inside you. That is what's referred to as "the living God."

The Midrash goes on to say that after all these events, Terah and his family settled in Haran.

SARAH, ABRAHAM'S WIFE

"Abraham married his niece Sarai, daughter of Haran. She was ten years younger than Abraham, but was no less righteous, and later even surpassed her spouse in the gift of prophecy."

Whenever the Midrash mentions any woman, it refers to "your inner woman" (whether you are a male or a female). Therefore, Sarai, who later became Sarah, symbolizes the desire to receive within you, which is your inner woman.

As long as the woman inside you exists without the right intention, she serves the destructive ego. But once the right intention is attached to her, the woman becomes a constructive force.

So it is here. "Abraham," the intention to bestow, marries Sarah, the desire to receive, and thus transforms her into a righteous woman. By unifying with Abraham, Sarah, the desire to receive, acquires the intention to bestow and becomes a pure and exalted state, and you begin to understand the meaning of true happiness, what it means to think about others instead of yourself, and what true love feels like.

Subsequently, Sarah becomes more exalted than Abraham because she contains an egoism that's absent in Abraham because he is inherently pure, the quality of *Bina* in you. Next, Sarah becomes the mother of all.

Abraham begins to attach the egoistic desires to himself and purify them. The first and closest desire to him is Sarah, followed by his students, whom we will discuss soon, then his sons—Isaac, Jacob—until you've achieved complete purification. As you've learned time and again, we're always talking about what is happening within you.

It is written about Sarah that "She later even surpassed her spouse in the gift of prophecy." There is no doubt about it because the Abraham in you is absolute bestowal and is therefore detached from egoism. Sarah, however, epitomizes your egoistic desire. Hence, in unifying with Abraham, she becomes a very significant figure (desire inside you).

Sarah is closer to the earth. It is written that she (as is every woman in our world) is not "detached from life," and at the same time she is connected to Abraham. This is why she can prophesy while being understood and admired.

But let us return to the Midrash. It is written, "By that time Abraham has turned exactly seventy..." This means that all seven *Sephirot* (*Hesed, Gevura, Tifferet, Netzah, Hod, Yesod,* and *Malchut*), the whole of Abraham, this entire desire within you, becomes corrected (by attaching to itself the previous degree of Terah, who believed in his son). And since each individual *Sephira* comprises 10 *Sephirot*, there are seventy in all.

THE TEACHER

For the first time, the Abraham inside you can begin to teach. Having unified with Sarah and reached the age of seventy, he finally became a fully functional desire. No longer was his head in the clouds, for Sarah "lowered him to the earth." Now you can connect with the people inside you and teach them without being considered eccentric. Now you will be understood.

Abraham passes the wisdom forward and thus connects to himself more desires and purifies them.

Here is what the Midrash has to say about the matter: "What did Abraham do in Haran? He called public gatherings and declared before them the truth about the one Creator, appealing to people to serve Him... In addition to public speeches, he held discussions in which he defended his claims against anyone who doubted them. He also composed books that proved the futility of idol-worshipping. Thus Abraham drew tens of thousands of followers, who accepted the existence of the Creator."

Indeed, this is precisely how Abraham gathers within you all the altruistic desires, which will later be called the "nation of Israel." "Israel" derives from the words *Yashar* (Heb. straight) and *El* (Heb. God), meaning straight to the Creator. Note that this notion has absolutely nothing to do with religion, nationality, or race. The nation of Israel (the desires aimed at the Creator) is formed within you (regardless of the denomination into which you were born).

Additionally, it is correctly written that "Abraham traveled the earth without rest, spreading the faith in the Creator." In other words, there is a continuous search for newer desires within you, which could be attached to the nation, i.e., corrected, whereby an altruistic intention will be added to an egoistic desire.

GO FORTH FROM YOUR COUNTRY

Dear reader, we have been navigating the "pages" of the Midrash for a while now, and with good reason. It is the only source to carefully detail the story of Abraham, from the moment when you barely feel him (his "birth") onward. The Midrash describes everything that happens to him until the moment when the Creator Himself addresses him.

But now we're returning to the written Torah (the Pentateuch. Midrash is the oral Torah). For the first time ever, the Creator directly addresses the Abraham within you because he can finally hear His instruction. Until now, you were different and incapable of perceiving it, and the Creator's instruction would have appeared unacceptable to you.

"Now the Lord said unto Abram: 'Go forth from your country, from your relatives and from the home of your father, to the land that I will show you, and I will make of you a great nation, and I will bless you, and make your name great; and you will be a blessing.'"

This is the start of your Abraham's journey with those desires he was able to attach to himself: Sarah, his household, and his students. The journey is "out of your country, away from your relatives and away from the home of your father." In other words, you must break away from all of it.

"Breaking away from the earth" means parting from all the desires that you still cannot correct. Their time will come, but for now you leave them behind and retain only those desires you can attach to *Bina*, the part of the Creator in you, this fervent will to bestow that you've acquired. You will need to take these desires and arrive with them at the spiritual level called the (First and Second) "Temple," the level of desires at which kings David and Solomon exist.

Jumping a bit ahead, I want to clarify that once you've attained their level—the complete correction of those desires you've "taken with you"—you will need to once again fall into the abyss of egoistic desires you have temporarily left behind. Having achieved correction, you will need to once again mingle with Nimrod, with Terah, and with Haran, for you will now have the strength to correct them.

Indeed, the purpose of your creation is the complete correction of all your desires. Only then will you merge with infinity and achieve the absolute bliss that exists even now, only you cannot feel it because of your uncorrected vessel.

It is written in the Torah, "Go forth from your country." That is, "Leave the place where you were born and have lived until now, reject your egoistic desires. Start developing above them, as though they do not exist."

That is followed by: "...and from your relatives and from the home of your father..." meaning "Part from your previous degree, leave behind your old environment that didn't engage in the spiritual pursuit."

"...to the land that I will show you." That is, "Make use of the desires that will awaken in you. They will be the desires you'll attach to your intention to bestow, called 'Abraham.'" The Creator will awaken these desires in you, and He will help you correct them. Thus He will lead you into the land of absolute bliss.

"And I will make of you a great nation, and I will bless you, and make your name great; and you will be a blessing."

What is the "great nation" spoken of here? There are numerous conjectures surrounding this "great nation." Some say this refers to the nation being chosen by God, but this is incorrect. In fact, this kind of separation and sense of superiority of one nation over another is precisely the root of all problems, as we can clearly see in our world.

However, everything becomes clear and takes its rightful place when we realize that the Torah speaks only about desires that exist within us. It follows that the notion of "great" refers to one who has reached the quality of bestowal and learned to truly love others. Therein lies true greatness. Once you grasp that concept, you will immediately wish to belong to this "nation." Indeed, the ultimate goal is to make the entire world "great."

"... and I will bless you ..."

What is a "blessing"? Whenever we receive a blessing in life, we are absolutely certain that it's given to keep us healthy, successful at our jobs, and so on. In truth, a blessing does not pertain to our egoistic world at all; it is a spiritual notion that leads us to the spiritual world. It has nothing to do with worldly affairs. A "blessing" is the force or Light that descends to us and corrects our intentions, transforming them from egoistic to altruistic.

Because you are connected to Abraham, you are granted this force. Once you have it, all the desires you've identified, those you've taken with you "from your country" and those you have yet to meet on your journey, are all corrected with this force called "blessing."

But let us continue. Look how harsh the following passage from the Midrash sounds: "I free you from the obligation to honor your father. You may leave him without a second thought. Your father and brother, who appear very friendly, are in fact hatching evil schemes. They're planning murder..." This reads like something straight out of a thriller.

But by now you know that the passage references your old states, which you've lived with before and which cannot agree with you. These desires see that you are right and thus admit that you have risen above them.

However, being the uncorrected desires that they are, the quality you propose them to live with seems like death. Therefore, sooner or later there will be a conflict in which some desires will have to be destroyed by others. When that time comes, you will have only one option—to separate yourself from these coarse egoistic desires to avoid quarreling with them.

Leaving them will preserve them for a time. They will remain, and you will live peacefully, only to return later and correct them. However, you will only return once you've gained sufficient strength and become a "great nation," capable of defeating (correcting) all the desires you have left behind.

The Creator does not reveal to Abraham where he will arrive at the end of his journey. "...to the land that I will show you," He says to him.

The desires to bestow that become revealed along the way, guiding you as they gradually manifest within, must be accepted in accordance with the law of bestowal, meaning with faith above reason. This means you mustn't pass them through your ego, meaning approach them with questions, "But what will this give me? It seems so illogical..."

The desires to bestow must be passed through your Abraham, the quality of bestowal within you. You must constantly identify with the quality of *Bina* within you, leaving all the egoistic thoughts by the wayside.

The Midrash says the following about Abraham: "He didn't ask the Creator a single question, like, 'How long will my journey take?'"

That is correct, because your ascension happens at the degree of Abraham (*Bina*) inside you, and at this degree you don't ask questions; you only ascend, breaking away from egoistic desires until you are strong enough to deal with them. But for now you are undergoing your very first correction.

The written Torah continues, "So Abram went, as the Lord had spoken unto him."

What does it mean, he "went"? It means you have begun to conquer the spiritual ladder. New egoistic desires keep popping up within you, which you can correct by attaching them to "Abraham." That is, you can view them through the prism of Abraham, constantly comparing them to Abraham's quality, thereby attaching them to him, to the quality of *Bina* in you. And so you will always be able to rise above them.

In Closing

Dear reader, we have come to the end of our book. We have examined two chapters: *Beresheet* (Genesis, Heb. In the beginning) and "Noah," and we have barely begun the chapter, "Go Forth."

Naturally, it is impossible to cover everything in such a short book, especially considering the fact that I had to keep the discourse fairly "light" to ensure that you understand it and are able to relate it to yourself. This book is for anyone who's only starting on the spiritual path.

For those who are already en route, there is the book, *The Zohar: annotations to the Ashlag commentary*, in which the explanation of the chapter *Beresheet* covers the entire book, and which presents the commentary of the great Kabbalist, Baal HaSulam. However, if you were to pick up that book today, you wouldn't understand a word of it, as it is written for those who already perceive the spiritual world and exist in both worlds, connecting them within.

If the desire to attain the spiritual world sincerely awakens in you, you will remain faithful to it. You will seek out any opportunity to preserve and cultivate this delicate bud within you, and you will surely achieve the desired goal.

Steadfast and tested guides await us on our path. Some of them we've already discovered within, while others are yet to be encountered, such as Moses and many more. We will pass through the "desert" (within), go down to "Egypt" (your ego), come out of it as "one nation" (strengthened altruistic desire), "wage war" (against the ego), fall only to rise again (succumb to the ego but press on toward spiritual attainment) until we finally reach the desire "straight to the Creator." So says the Torah, the book that's never been wrong.

About the Author

Semion Vinokur is a prolific script writer and director. He has directed and written for at least seventy documentaries, and eleven feature films. He is the chairman of the School for Talented Young Cinematographers in the Israeli Ministry of Absorption, and is currently in charge of the student's graduation projects at "Sapir" film Academy.

Many of Mr. Vinokur's films (producing, script writing and directing) were awarded and screened in major International film festivals in the United States, Italy, Israel, Russia, China, Argentina, and many other countries.

Mr. Vinokur's films have won numerous awards. He won The Gold Medal at Flagstaff International Film Festival (*What fire can't burn*), The Bronze Plaque at The Columbus International Film & Video Festival (*Kalik in Black, White, and Color*), First Prize at the Shanghai International Documentary Film Festival (*Magnolia*), a special award at the *National Geographic International Film Contest* for his short film, *Toward Integral Consciousness*, and many more.

Semion Vinokur is also the author of the celebrated cinematic novel, *The Kabbalist*.

Further Reading

To help you determine which book you would like to read next, we have divided the books into six categories—Beginners, Intermediate, Advanced, Good for All, Textbooks, and For Children. The first three categories are divided by the level of prior knowledge readers are required to have in order to easily relate to the book. The fourth category, Good for All, includes books you can always enjoy, whether you are a complete novice or well versed in Kabbalah.

The fifth category, Textbooks, includes translations of authentic source materials from earlier Kabbalists, such as the Ari, Rav Yehuda Ashlag (Baal HaSulam) and his son and successor, Rav Baruch Ashlag (the Rabash). The category, For Children, includes books that are suitable for children ages 3 and above. Those are not Kabbalah books per se, but are rather inspired by the teaching and convey the Kabbalistic message of love and unity.

Additional material can be found at www.kabbalah.info. All materials on this site, including e-versions of published books, can be downloaded free of charge.

GOOD FOR ALL

The Kabbalist: a cinematic novel

At the dawn of the deadliest era in human history, the 20th century, a mysterious man appeared carrying a stern warning for humanity and an unlikely solution to its suffering. In his writings, Kabbalist Yehuda Ashlag described in clarity and great detail the wars and upheavals he foresaw, and even more strikingly, the current economic, political, and social crises we are facing today. His deep yearning for a united humanity has driven him to unlock *The Book of Zohar* and make it—and the unique force contained therein—accessible to all.

The Kabbalist is a cinematic novel that will turn on its head everything you thought you knew about Kabbalah, spirituality, freedom of will, and our perception of reality. The book carries a message of unity with scientific clarity and poetic depth. It transcends religion, nationality, mysticism, and the fabric of space and time to show us that the only miracle is the one taking place within, when we begin to act in harmony with Nature and with the entire humanity.

The Point in the Heart: A Source of Delight for My Soul

The Point in the Heart; a Source of Delight for My Soul is a unique collection of excerpts from a man whose wisdom has earned him devoted students in North America and the world over. Michael Laitman is a scientist, a Kabbalist, and a great thinker who presents ancient wisdom in a compelling style.

This book does not profess to teach Kabbalah, but rather gently introduces ideas from the teaching. *The Point in the Heart* is a window to a new perception. As the author himself testifies to the wisdom of Kabbalah, "It is a science of emotion, a science of pleasure. You are welcome to open and to taste."

Attaining the Worlds Beyond

From the introduction to *Attaining the Worlds Beyond*: "Not feeling well on the Jewish New Year's Eve of September 1991, my teacher called me to his bedside and handed me his notebook, saying, 'Take it and learn from it.' The following morning, he perished in my arms, leaving me and many of his other disciples without guidance in this world."

"He used to say, 'I want to teach you to turn to the Creator, rather than to me, because He is the only strength, the only Source of all that exists, the only one who can really help you, and He awaits your prayers for help. When you seek help in your search for freedom from the bondage of this world, help in elevating yourself above this world, help in finding the self, and help in determining your purpose in life, you must turn to the Creator, who sends you all those aspirations in order to compel you to turn to Him.'"

Attaining the Worlds Beyond holds within it the content of that notebook, as well as other inspiring texts. This book reaches out to all those seekers who want to find a logical, reliable way to understand the world we live in. This fascinating introduction to the wisdom of Kabbalah will enlighten the mind, invigorate the heart, and move readers to the depths of their souls.

Bail Yourself Out

Bail Yourself Out: how you can emerge strong from the world crisis introduces several extraordinary concepts that weave into a complete solution: 1) The global crisis is essentially not financial, but *psychological*: People have stopped trusting each other, and where there is no trust there is no trade, but only war, isolation, and pain. 2) This mistrust is a result of a *natural process* that's been evolving for millennia and is culminating today. 3) To resolve the crisis, we must first *understand* the process that created the alienation. 4) The first, and most important, step to understanding the crisis is to *inform* people about this natural process through books, such as *Bail Yourself Out*, TV, cinema, and any other means of communication. 5) With this information, we will "*revamp*" our relationships and build them on trust, collaboration, and most importantly, care. This mending process will guarantee that we and our families will prosper in a world of plenty.

Basic Concepts in Kabbalah

This is a book to help readers cultivate an *approach to the concepts* of Kabbalah, to spiritual objects, and to spiritual terms. By reading and re-reading in this book, one develops internal observations, senses, and approaches that did not previously exist within. These newly acquired observations are like sensors that "feel" the space around us that is hidden from our ordinary senses.

Basic Concepts in Kabbalah is intended to foster contemplation of spiritual terms. Once we are integrated with these terms, we can begin to see the unveiling of the spiritual structure that surrounds us, almost as if a mist has been lifted. It is a book for those who wish to awaken the deepest and subtlest sensations they can possess.

Children of Tomorrow: Guidelines for Raising Happy Children in the 21st Century

Children of Tomorrow is a new beginning for you and your children. The big revelation is that raising kids is all about games and play, relating to them as small grownups, and making all major decisions together. You will be surprised to discover how teaching kids about positive things like friendship and caring for others automatically spills into other areas of our lives through the day.

Open any page and you will find thought-provoking quotes about every aspect of children's lives: parent-children relations, friendships and conflicts, and a clear picture of how schools should be designed and function.

The Wise Heart: Tales and allegories by three contemporary sages

Kabbalah students and enthusiasts in Kabbalah often wonder what the spiritual world actually feels like to a Kabbalist. The Wise Heart is a lovingly crafted anthology comprised of tales and allegories by Kabbalist Dr. Michael Laitman, his mentor, Rav Baruch Ashlag (Rabash), and Rabash's father and mentor, Rav Yehuda Ashlag, author of the acclaimed Sulam (Ladder) commentary on The Book of Zohar. The poems herein offer surprising and often amusing depictions of human nature, with a loving and tender touch that is truly unique to Kabbalists.

FOR CHILDREN

Together Forever: The story about the magician who didn't want to be alone

Like all good children's stories, *Together Forever* transcends boundaries of age, culture, and upbringing. Here, the author tells us that if we are patient and endure the trials we encounter along our life's path, we will become stronger, braver, and wiser.

In this warm, tender tale, Michael Laitman shares with children and parents alike some of the gems and charms of the spiritual world. The wisdom of Kabbalah is filled with spellbinding stories. *Together Forever* is yet another gift from this ageless source of wisdom, whose lessons make our lives richer, easier, and far more fulfilling.

Miracles Can Happen: Tales for children, but not only...

"*Miracles Can Happen*," Princes Peony," and "Mary and the Paints" are only three of ten beautiful stories for children ages 3-10. Written especially for children, these short tales convey a single message of love, unity, and care for all beings. The unique illustrations were carefully crafted to contribute to the overall message of the book, and a child who's heard or read any story in this collection is guaranteed to go to sleep smiling.

The Baobab that Opened Its Heart: and Other Nature Tales for Children

The Baobab that Opened Its Heart is a collection of stories for children, but not just for them. The stories in this collection were written with the love of Nature, of people, and specifically with children in mind. They all share the desire to tell nature's tale of unity, connectedness, and love.

Kabbalah teaches that love is nature's guiding force, the reason for creation. The stories in this book convey it in the unique way that Kabbalah engenders in its students. The variety of authors and diversity of styles allows each reader to find the story that they like most.

BEGINNERS

A Glimpse of Light:
The Basics of the Wisdom of Kabbalah

A Glimpse of Light: The Basics of the Wisdom of Kabbalah offers selected contemplations from the ocean of wisdom contained in the wisdom of Kabbalah. This book touches upon topics such as pleasure, ego, love, men and women, globalization, education, ecology, Nature, perception of reality, The Book of Zohar, and spirituality. Just open the book wherever you wish, and begin to read. Each chapter contains several sections that combine to form a complete picture. This collection will serve you as a "glimpse of the Light," a window into the profound emotions and perceptions we can all attain by studying the wisdom of Kabbalah.

The Spiritual Roots of the Holy Land

The Spiritual Roots of the Holy Land takes you on a wondrous journey through the land of Israel. As you take in the breathtaking pictures of the holy land, another layer of the age-old country is revealed—its spiritual roots, the ebb and flow of forces that have shaped the curvy landscape that is sacred to billions of people around the world. At the end of the book, you'll find roadmaps of Israel, to help you locate each place you visit, whether in mind or in body, and more details on the forefathers who have made this land the focal point of an entire planet.

Self-Interest vs. Altruism in the Global Era: How society can turn self-interests into mutual benefit

Self-Interest vs. Altruism in the Global Era presents a new perspective on the world's challenges, regarding them as necessary consequences of humanity's growing egotism, rather than a series of errors. In that spirit, the book suggests ways to use our egos for society's benefit, rather than trying to suppress them.

...Stating that society's future relies on cooperation of people to work together for society, stating that much of society's degradation in recent decades has been the result of narcissism and greed, Self Interest vs. Altruism is a curious and recommended read.

James A. Cox, Editor-in-Chief, *Midwest Book Review*

A Guide to the Hidden Wisdom of Kabbalah

A Guide to the Hidden Wisdom of Kabbalah is a light and reader-friendly guide to beginners in Kabbalah, covering everything from the history of Kabbalah to how this wisdom can help resolve the world crisis.

The book is set up in three parts: Part 1 covers the history, facts, and fallacies about Kabbalah, and introduces its key concepts. Part 2 tells you all about the spiritual worlds and other neat stuff like the meaning of letters and the power of music. Part 3 covers the implementation of Kabbalah at a time of world crisis.

Kabbalah Revealed: A Guide to a More Peaceful Life

This is the most clearly written, reader-friendly guide to making sense of the surrounding world. Each of its six chapters focuses on a different aspect of the wisdom of Kabbalah, illuminating its teachings and explaining them using various examples from our day-to-day lives.

The first three chapters in Kabbalah Revealed explain why the world is in a state of crisis, how our growing desires promote progress as well as alienation, and why the biggest deterrent to achieving positive change is rooted in our own spirits. Chapters Four through Six offer a prescription for positive change. In these chapters, we learn how we can use our spirits to build a personally peaceful life in harmony with all of Creation.

Wondrous Wisdom

This book offers an initial course on Kabbalah. Like all the books presented here, Wondrous Wisdom is based solely on authentic teachings passed down from Kabbalist teacher to student over thousands of years. At the heart of the book is a sequence of lessons revealing the nature of Kabbalah's wisdom and explaining how to attain it. For every person questioning 'Who am I really?' and 'Why am I on this planet?' this book is a must.

Awakening to Kabbalah: The Guiding Light of Spiritual Fulfillment

A distinctive, personal, and awe-filled introduction to an ancient wisdom tradition. In this book, Rav Laitman offers a deeper understanding of the fundamental teachings of

Kabbalah, and how you can use its wisdom to clarify your relationship with others and the world around you.

Using language both scientific and poetic, he probes the most profound questions of spirituality and existence. This provocative, unique guide will inspire and invigorate you to see beyond the world as it is and the limitations of your everyday life, become closer to the Creator, and reach new depths of the soul.

Kabbalah, Science, and the Meaning of Life

Science explains the mechanisms that sustain life; Kabbalah explains why life exists. *Kabbalah, Science, and the Meaning of Life* combines science and spirituality in a captivating dialogue that reveals life's meaning.

For centuries, Kabbalists have been writing that the world is a single entity divided into separate beings. Today the cutting-edge science of quantum physics states a very similar idea: that at the most fundamental level of matter, we are all literally one.

Science proves that reality is affected by the observer who examines it; and so does Kabbalah. But Kabbalah makes an even bolder statement: even the Creator, the Maker of reality, is within the observer.

These earthshaking concepts and more are eloquently introduced so that even readers new to Kabbalah or science will easily understand them. So if you are curious about why you are here, what life means, and what you can do to enjoy it more, this book is for you.

From Chaos to Harmony

Many researchers and scientists agree that the ego is the reason behind the perilous state our world is in today. Laitman's groundbreaking book not only demonstrates that egoism has been the basis for all suffering throughout human history, but also shows how we can turn our plight to pleasure.

The book contains a clear analysis of the human soul and its problems, and provides a "roadmap" of what we need to do to once again be happy. *From Chaos to Harmony* explains how we can rise to a new level of existence on personal, social, national, and international levels.

Kabbalah for Beginners

Kabbalah for Beginners is a book for all those seeking answers to life's essential questions. We all want to know why we are here, why there is pain, and how we can make life more enjoyable. The four parts of this book provide us with reliable answers to these questions, as well as clear explanations of the gist of Kabbalah and its practical implementations.

Part One discusses the discovery of the wisdom of Kabbalah, and how it was developed, and finally concealed until our time. Part Two introduces the gist of the wisdom of Kabbalah, using ten easy drawings to help us understand the structure of the spiritual worlds, and how they relate to our world. Part Three reveals Kabbalistic concepts that are largely unknown to the public, and Part Four elaborates on practical means you and I can take, to make our lives better and more enjoyable for us and for our children.

INTERMEDIATE

The Kabbalah Experience

The depth of the wisdom revealed in the questions and answers within this book will inspire readers to reflect and contemplate. This is not a book to race through, but rather one that should be read thoughtfully and carefully. With this approach, readers will begin to experience a growing sense of enlightenment while simply absorbing the answers to the questions every Kabbalah student asks along the way.

The Kabbalah Experience is a guide from the past to the future, revealing situations that all students of Kabbalah will experience at some point along their journeys. For those who cherish every moment in life, this book offers unparalleled insights into the timeless wisdom of Kabbalah.

The Path of Kabbalah

This unique book combines beginners' material with more advanced concepts and teachings. If you have read a book or two of Laitman's, you will find this book very easy to relate to.

While touching upon basic concepts such as perception of reality and Freedom of Choice, *The Path of Kabbalah* goes deeper and expands beyond the scope of beginners' books. The structure of the worlds, for example, is explained in greater detail here than in the "pure" beginners' books. Also described is the spiritual root of mundane matters such as the Hebrew calendar and the holidays.

ADVANCED

The Science of Kabbalah

Kabbalist and scientist Rav Michael Laitman, PhD, designed this book to introduce readers to the special language and terminology of the authentic wisdom of Kabbalah. Here, Rav Laitman reveals authentic Kabbalah in a manner both rational and mature. Readers are gradually led to understand the logical design of the Universe and the life that exists in it.

The Science of Kabbalah, a revolutionary work unmatched in its clarity, depth, and appeal to the intellect, will enable readers to approach the more technical works of Baal HaSulam (Rabbi Yehuda Ashlag), such as *The Study of the Ten Sefirot* and *The Book of Zohar*. Readers of this book will enjoy the satisfying answers to the riddles of life that only authentic Kabbalah provides. Travel through the pages and prepare for an astonishing journey into the Upper Worlds.

Introduction to the Book of Zohar

This volume, along with *The Science of Kabbalah*, is a required preparation for those who wish to understand the hidden message of *The Book of Zohar*. Among the many helpful topics dealt with in this text is an introduction to the "language of roots and branches," without which the stories in *The Zohar* are mere fable and legend. *Introduction to the Book of Zohar* will provide readers with the necessary tools to understand authentic Kabbalah as it was originally meant to be—as a means to attain the Upper Worlds.

The Book of Zohar: annotations to the Ashlag commentary

The Book of Zohar is an age-old source of wisdom and the basis for all Kabbalistic literature. Since its appearance, it has been the primary, and often only source used by Kabbalists.

Written in a unique and metaphorical language, The Book of Zohar enriches our understanding of reality and widens our worldview. Rav Yehuda Ashlag's unique Sulam (Ladder) commentary allows us to grasp the hidden meanings of the text and "climb" toward the lucid perceptions and insights that the book holds for those who study it.

TEXTBOOKS

Shamati (I Heard)

Rav Michael Laitman's words on the book: "Among all the texts and notes that were used by my teacher, Rav Baruch Shalom Halevi Ashlag (the Rabash), there was one special notebook he always carried. This notebook contained transcripts of his conversations with his father, Rav Yehuda Leib Halevi Ashlag (Baal HaSulam), author of the Sulam (Ladder) commentary on The Book of Zohar, The Study of the Ten Sefirot (a commentary on the texts of the Kabbalist, Ari), and many other works on Kabbalah.

"Not feeling well on the Jewish New Year's Eve of September 1991, the Rabash summoned me to his bedside and handed me a notebook, whose cover contained only one word, Shamati (I Heard). As he handed the notebook, he said, 'Take it and learn from it.' The following morning, my teacher perished in my arms, leaving me and many of his other disciples without guidance in this world.

Committed to Rabash's legacy to disseminate the wisdom of Kabbalah, I published the notebook just as it was written, thus retaining the text's transforming powers. Among all the books of Kabbalah, *Shamati* is a unique and compelling creation."

Kabbalah for the Student

Kabbalah for the Student offers authentic texts by Rav Yehuda Ashlag, author of the *Sulam* (Ladder) commentary on *The Book of Zohar*, his son and successor, Rav Baruch Ashlag, as well as other great Kabbalists. It also offers illustrations that accurately depict the evolution of the Upper Worlds as Kabbalists experience them. The book also contains several explanatory essays that help us understand the texts within.

In *Kabbalah for the Student*, Rav Michael Laitman, PhD, Rav Baruch Ashlag's personal assistant and prime student, compiled all the texts a Kabbalah student would need in order to attain the spiritual worlds. In his daily lessons, Rav Laitman bases his teaching on these inspiring texts, thus helping novices and veterans alike to better understand the spiritual path we undertake on our fascinating journey to the Higher Realms.

Rabash—the Social Writings

Rav Baruch Shalom HaLevi Ashlag (Rabash) played a remarkable role in the history of Kabbalah. He provided us with the necessary final link connecting the wisdom of Kabbalah to our human experience. His father and teacher was the great Kabbalist, Rav Yehuda Leib HaLevi Ashlag, known as Baal HaSulam for his *Sulam* (Ladder) commentary on *The Book of Zohar*. Yet, if not for the essays of Rabash, his father's efforts to disclose the wisdom of Kabbalah to all would have been in vain. Without those essays, few would be able to achieve the spiritual attainment that Baal HaSulam so desperately wanted us to obtain.

The writings in this book aren't just for reading. They are more like an experiential user's guide. It is very important to work with them in order to see what they truly contain. The reader should try to put them into practice by living out the emotions Rabash so masterfully describes. He always advised his students to summarize the articles, to work with the texts, and those who attempt it discover that it always yields new insights. Thus, readers are advised to work with the texts, summarize them, translate them, and implement them in the group. Those who do so will discover the power in the writings of Rabash.

Gems of Wisdom: words of the great Kabbalists from all generations

Through the millennia, Kabbalists have bequeathed us with numerous writings. In their compositions, they have laid out a structured method that can lead, step by step, unto a world of eternity and wholeness.

Gems of Wisdom is a collection of selected excerpts from the writings of the greatest Kabbalists from all generations, with particular emphasis on the writings of Rav Yehuda Leib HaLevi Ashlag (Baal HaSulam), author of the *Sulam* [Ladder] commentary of *The Book of Zohar*.

The sections have been arranged by topics, to provide the broadest view possible on each topic. This book is a useful guide to any person desiring spiritual advancement.

Let There Be Light: selected excerpts from The Book of Zohar

The *Zohar* contains all the secrets of Creation, but until recently the wisdom of Kabbalah was locked under a thousand locks. Thanks to the work of Rav Yehuda Ashlag (1884-1954), the last of the great Kabbalists, *The Zohar* is revealed today in order to propel humanity to its next degree.

Let There Be Light contains selected excerpts from the series *Zohar for All*, a refined edition of *The Book of Zohar* with the *Sulam* commentary. Each piece was carefully chosen for its beauty and depth as well as its capacity to draw the reader into *The Zohar* and get the most out of the reading experience. As *The Zohar* speaks of nothing but the intricate web that connects all souls, diving into its words attracts the special force that exists in that state of oneness, where we are all connected.

CONTACT INFORMATION

1057 Steeles Avenue West, Suite 532
Toronto, ON, M2R 3X1
Canada

Bnei Baruch USA,
2009 85th street, #51,
Brooklyn, New York, 11214
USA

E-mail: info@kabbalah.info
Web site: www.kabbalah.info

Toll free in USA and Canada:
1-866-LAITMAN
Fax: 1-905 886 9697